BUDDHISM FOR BEGINNERS

Also by Thubten Chodron

Blossoms of the Dharma: Living as a Buddhist Nun
(North Atlantic Books, Berkeley CA)

Choosing Simplicity
by Venerable Master Wu Yin,
ed. by Thubten Chodron
(Snow Lion Publications, Ithaca NY)

Interfaith Insights
(Timeless Books, New Delhi)

Open Heart, Clear Mind
(Snow Lion Publications, Ithaca NY)

Taming the Monkey Mind
(Heian International, Torrance CA)

Transforming the Heart: The Buddhist Way to Joy and Courage,
by Geshe Jampa Tegchok, ed. by Thubten Chodron
(Snow Lion Publications, Ithaca NY)

BUDDHISM FOR BEGINNERS

by Thubten Chodron

Snow Lion Publications
Ithaca, New York

Snow Lion Publications
605 West State Street
P. O. Box 6483
Ithaca, NY 14851 USA
(607) 273-8519
www.snowlionpub.com

Copyright © 2001 Thubten Chodron

Printed in Canada on acid-free, recycled paper.

ISBN 1-55939-153-7

Library of Congress Cataloging-in-Publication Data
Thubten Chodron, 1950-
Buddhism for Beginners / by Thubten Chodron
p. cm.
Includes bibliographical references.
ISBN 1-55939-153-7 (alk. paper)
1. Buddhism -- Doctrines. I. Title.
BQ4022 .T48 2001
294.3 -- dc21

00-011611

CONTENTS

THE DALAI LAMA

FOREWORD

I am happy to know about this book, *Buddhism for Beginners,* by Thubten Chodron. This book is written mainly for people wanting to understand basic Buddhist principles and how to integrate them into their lives. It might be useful if I mention a few words here about what should be their approach to Buddhism. In the beginning one should remain skeptical and rely on questioning and checking the teachings based on one's understanding. One can then have trust and confidence in the teachings. Buddha himself suggested this approach when he told his followers to accept his teaching after due analysis, and not merely out of respect and faith. Hence it is important to know that the main cause of faith is reflecting on reasons. This promotes conviction and helps develop actual experience. As one thinks more and more upon reasonings, one's ascertainment increases, and this in turn, induces experience, whereby faith becomes more firm.

His Holiness the Fourteenth Dalai Lama

INTRODUCTION

I had been in Singapore just a few days when a young man appeared at my door. "Can I ask you some questions about Buddhism?" he queried. We sat down and began to talk. Some of his questions were those also asked by Westerners new to Buddhism. Others were unique to Asians who had grown up in societies where Buddhism and the old folk religions were often mixed, at least in the minds of the general population. As I began teaching in Singapore, I noticed that many people had the same questions.

Soon thereafter, another man came to see me, and in the course of our discussion he said, "We need to hear about the Buddha's teachings in everyday English, a clear explanation without a lot of Pali and Sanskrit terms that we don't understand. Please write a book that will help us. I'd be happy to help you."

The idea for this book came from these two people: Lee Siew Cheung and Robert Gwee. It was initially printed privately in Singapore by Amitabha Buddhist Centre in 1988 and was entitled *I Wonder Why*. As people read it, they sent me more questions, which are included in the present edition.

Asking questions is healthy. It enables us to clarify doubts and gain new information. Many people have similar questions, and asking our questions is generally appreciated by fellow students who were too shy to ask! However, I believe that spiritual practice is more about holding questions than finding answers. Seeking one correct answer often comes from a wish to make life—which is basically fluid—into something certain and fixed. This often leads to rigidity, closed-mindedness, and intolerance. On the other hand, holding a question—exploring its many facets over time—puts us in touch with the mystery of life. Holding questions accustoms us to the ungraspable nature of life and enables us to understand things from a range of perspectives. Thus, although answers are seemingly given to questions in this book, we must contemplate both, turning them over again and again so we see them from many sides and integrate them into our lives.

This book is designed for people who are interested in Buddhism as well as those who have studied or practiced it for years but are still unclear about some points. The way some of the initial material on Buddhism was translated in the West decades ago has led to misinterpretations even among those who teach Buddhism at the high school and college levels. I hope that this book will help those teachers and their students.

You can read this book from cover to cover or go directly to the sections that interest you. This book is not designed to be a comprehensive introduction to Buddhism, but to clarify points, provide Buddhist perspectives on modern issues, and stimulate the curiosity and questioning minds of the readers.

Appreciation

My deepest respect and gratitude are offered to the Buddhas. I would like to thank all of my teachers, in particular His Holiness the Dalai Lama, Tsenzhab Serkong Rinpoche, and Zopa Rinpoche, for their teachings and guidance. I appreciate the members of Amitabha Buddhist Center in Singapore and Dharma Friendship Foundation in Seattle for their inspiration and help in writing this book. Special thanks go to Monica Faulkner for her help in editing the manuscript. All errors are my own.

Technical Notes

"He" and "she" are used interchangeably for the third person pronoun. "Mind," "mindstream," and "consciousness" are used interchangeably to refer to the part of us that perceives and experiences.

This includes what we call "heart" in the West. In Buddhism, one word encompasses the meaning of heart and mind. "The Buddha" refers to the historical Buddha, Shakyamuni, who lived in India over 2,500 years ago. "Buddhas" refers to all enlightened beings, of whom Shakyamuni is one.

I have tried to define Buddhist terms as they arise in the text. A glossary at the end of the book is also provided.

Thubten Chodron
Seattle, WA
June 16, 2000

Chapter One

THE ESSENCE OF BUDDHISM

What is the essence of the Buddha's teachings?

Simply speaking, it is to avoid harming others and to help them as much as possible. Another way of expressing this is the oft-quoted verse:

> Abandon negative action;
> Create perfect virtue;
> Subdue your own mind.
> This is the teaching of the Buddha.

By abandoning negative actions, such as hurting others, and destructive motivations, such as anger, attachment, and closed-mindedness, we stop harming ourselves and others. By creating perfect virtue, we develop beneficial attitudes, such as equanimity, love, compassion, and joy, and act constructively. By subduing our minds and understanding reality, we leave behind all false projections, thus making ourselves calm and peaceful.

We can also speak of the essence of the Buddha's teachings as they are explained in the Four Noble Truths: the truth of suffering, the cause of suffering, the cessation of suffering and its causes, and the path to that cessation. When Buddha spoke about suffering, he meant that we have unsatisfactory experiences. Even the happiness we have does not last forever, and that situation is unsatisfactory. The causes of our problems lie not in the external environment and those inhabiting it, but in our own mind. The disturbing attitudes and negative emotions, such as clinging attachment, anger, and ignorance are the real source of our unhappiness. Since these are based on misconceptions about the nature of reality, they can be removed from our mindstream. We then abide in the blissful state of nirvana, which is the absence of all unsatisfactory experiences and their causes. A path exists to realize reality and increase our good qualities. The Buddha described this path, and we have the ability to actualize it.

The path is often described by the Three Higher Trainings: Ethical Discipline, Meditative Stabilization, and Wisdom. First, we must become a good human being who functions well in society and lives harmoniously with others. The Higher Training of Ethical Discipline enables us to do this. Because our actions and speech are now calmer, we can proceed to tame the mind by developing single-pointed concentration or the Higher Training of Meditative Stabilization. This leads us to cut the root of suffering, the ignorance grasping at inherent existence, and for this we develop the Higher Training in Wisdom, so that we can perceive reality as it is.

The Three Higher Trainings can be subdivided into the Noble Eight-fold Path. Ethical Discipline includes: 1) right speech: true, kind, and appropriate speech; 2) right activity: actions which do not harm others; and 3) right livelihood: obtaining our subsistence—food, clothing, and so forth—by non-harmful and honest means. The Higher Training of Meditative Stabilization includes: 4) right effort: effort to counteract the disturbing attitudes and negative emotions by meditating on the path; 5) right mindfulness: counteracting laxity and excitement in our meditation; and 6) right samadhi: the mind that can remain fixed one-pointedly upon virtuous objects. The Higher Training of Wisdom includes: 7) right view: the wisdom realizing emptiness, and 8) right thought: the mind that can explain the path clearly to others and is motivated by the wish for them to be free from suffering.

The essence of the Buddhist path is also contained in the three principal aspects of the path: the determination to be free, the altruistic intention (bodhicitta), and the wisdom realizing reality. Initially, we must have the determination to be free from the confusion of our problems and their causes. Then, seeing that other people also have problems, with love and compassion we will develop an altruistic intention to become a Buddha so that we will be capable of helping others most effectively. To do this, we must develop the wisdom that understands the true nature of ourselves and other phenomena and thus eliminates all false projections.

What is the goal of the Buddhist path?

The Buddhist path leads us to discover a state of lasting happiness for both ourselves and others by freeing ourselves from cyclic existence, the cycle of constantly recurring problems that we experience at present. We are born and die under the influence of ignorance, disturbing attitudes, and contaminated actions (karma). Although all of us want to be happy, and we try hard to get the things that will make us happy, no one is totally satisfied with his or her life. And although we all want to be free from difficulties, problems come our way without our even trying. People may have many good things going for them in their lives, but when we talk with them for more than five minutes, they start telling us their problems. Those of us who are in this situation, who are not yet Buddhas, are called "sentient beings."

The root cause of cyclic existence is ignorance: we do not understand who we are, how we exist or how other phenomena exist. Unaware of our own ignorance, we project fantasized ways of existing onto ourselves and others, thinking that everyone and everything has some inherent nature and exists independently, in and of itself. This gives rise to attachment, an attitude that exaggerates the good qualities of people and things or superimposes good qualities that are not there and then clings to those people or things, thinking they will bring us real happiness. When things do not work out as we expected or wished they would, or when something interferes with our happiness, we become angry. These three basic disturbing attitudes—ignorance, attachment, and anger—give rise to a host of other ones, such as jealousy, pride, and resentment. These attitudes then motivate us to act, speak, or think. Such actions leave imprints on our mindstreams, and these imprints then influence what we will experience in the future.

We are liberated from the cycle of rebirth by generating the wisdom realizing emptiness or selflessness. This wisdom is a profound realization of the lack of a solid, independent essence in ourselves, others, and everything that exists. It eliminates all ignorance, wrong conceptions, disturbing attitudes, and negative emotions, thus putting a stop to all misinformed or contaminated actions. The state of being liberated is called nirvana or liberation. All beings have the potential to attain liberation, a state of lasting happiness.

What are the Three Jewels? How do we relate to them? What does it mean to take refuge in the Three Jewels?

The Three Jewels are the Buddha, Dharma and Sangha. A Buddha is one who has purified all the defilements of the mind—the disturbing attitudes, negative emotions and their seeds, the imprints of the actions motivated by them, and the stains of these disturbing attitudes and negative emotions. A Buddha has also developed all good qualities, such as impartial love and compassion, profound wisdom, and skillful means of guiding others. The Dharma is the preventive measures that keep us from problems and suffering. This includes the teachings of the Buddha and the beneficial mental states that practicing the teachings leads to. The Sangha are those beings who have direct nonconceptual understanding of reality. Sangha can also refer to the community of ordained people who practice Buddha's teachings, but this sangha is the conventional representation of the Sangha Jewel, and is not the one we take refuge in.

Our relationship to the Three Jewels is analogous to a sick person who seeks help from a doctor, medicine, and nurses. We suffer from various unsatisfactory circumstances in our lives. The Buddha is like a doctor who correctly diagnoses the cause of our problems and prescribes the appropriate medicine. The Dharma is our real refuge, the medicine that cures our problems and their causes. By helping us along the path, the Sangha is like the nurse who assists us in taking the medicine.

Taking refuge means relying wholeheartedly on the Three Jewels to inspire and guide us toward a constructive and beneficial direction in our lives. Taking refuge does not mean passively hiding under the protection of the Buddha, Dharma, and Sangha. Rather, it is an active process of moving in the direction that they show us and thus improving the quality of our life.

When people take refuge, they clarify to themselves what direction they are taking in life, who is guiding them, and who their companions are on the path. This eliminates the indecision and confusion arising from uncertainty about their spiritual path. Some people window-shop for spirituality: Monday they use crystals, Tuesday they do channeling, Wednesday they do Hindu meditation, Thursday they do Hatha Yoga, Friday they have holistic healing, Saturday they do Buddhist meditation, and Sunday they use Tarot cards. They learn a lot about many things, but their attachment, anger, and closed-mindedness don't change much. Taking refuge is making a clear decision about what our principal path is. Nevertheless, it is possible to practice the Buddha's teachings and to benefit from them without taking refuge or becoming a Buddhist.

Must we be a Buddhist to practice what the Buddha taught?

No. The Buddha gave a wide variety of instructions, and if some of them help us live to better, to solve our problems and become kinder, then we are free to practice them. There is no need to call ourselves Buddhists. The purpose of the Buddha's teachings is to benefit us, and if putting some of them into practice helps us live more peacefully with ourselves and others, that is what's important.

Chapter Two

THE BUDDHA

Who is the Buddha? If he is just a man, how can he help us?

There are many ways to describe who the Buddha is. These various perspectives have their sources in the Buddha's teachings. One is as the historical Buddha, a human being who lived 2,500 years ago and who cleansed his mind of all defilements and developed all of his potential. Any being who does likewise is also considered a Buddha, for there are many Buddhas, not just one. Another way is to understand a particular Buddha or Buddhist deity as all the enlightened minds manifesting in a particular physical aspect in order to communicate with us. Yet another way is to see the Buddha or any of the enlightened Buddhist deities as the appearance of the Buddha that we will become once we have completely cleansed our minds of defilements and developed all of our potential. Let's examine each of these in more depth.

The Historical Buddha

The historical Buddha Shakyamuni was born as Prince Siddhartha Gautama in an area near the present border between India and Nepal. He had all that life could offer: material possessions, a loving family, fame, reputation and power. Soon after his birth, a soothe-sayer predicted that Siddhartha would become either a great king or a great spiritual leader. Wanting him to be a great political leader, his father protected him from any contact with unpleasant situations. However, the young Siddhartha sneaked out of the palace and on his forays in the town witnessed first a sick person, then a old one, and finally a corpse. He became disillusioned with things that brought temporary, worldly happiness but did not solve the basic human predicament. On another excursion into town, he saw a wandering ascetic and learned that this person was seeking liberation from the cycle of existence to which he was bound by ignorance and karma. Siddhartha then left his princely life to become an ascetic, searching for truth. After six years of severe physical austerity, he realized that extreme self-denial was not the path to ultimate happiness. He gave up his extreme ascetic practices, and sitting under the bodhi tree, near present-day Bodhgaya, India, he entered into a deep meditation in which he completely purified his mind of all wrong conceptions and defilements and perfected all of his potential and good qualities. He then proceeded to teach with compassion, wisdom, and skill for forty-five years. In this way, he enabled others to gradually purify their minds, develop their potential, and attain the same realizations and state of happiness that he had. Thus, the word *Buddha* means "the awakened one," one who has purified and developed his or her mind completely.

How can such a person save us from our problems and pain? The Buddha cannot pull the disturbing attitudes of ignorance, anger, and attachment from our minds in the same way as a thorn can be pulled from our foot. Nor can the Buddha wash away our defilements with water or pour realizations into our minds. The Buddha has impartial compassion for all sentient beings and cherishes them more than himself, so if he could have eliminated our suffering by his actions, the Buddha would have done so.

However, our experiences of happiness and pain depend on our minds. They depend on whether or not we subdue our disturbing attitudes and contaminated actions (karma). The Buddha showed us the method to do this, the method that he himself used to go from the state of an ordinary confused being—the way we are now—to the state of total purification and growth, or Buddhahood. It is up to us to practice this method and transform our own minds. Shakyamuni Buddha is someone who did what we want to do—he reached a state of lasting happiness. His example and teachings indicate how we can do the same. But the Buddha can't control our minds; only we can do that. Our enlightenment depends not only on the Buddha showing us the way, but also on our own efforts to follow it.

To use an analogy, suppose we want to go to London. First we find out if a place called London actually exists. Then we look for someone who has been there and who has the knowledge, capability, and willingness to give us all of the travel information. Following someone who had never been there would be foolish, because that person could unwittingly give us mistaken information. Likewise, the Buddha has attained enlightenment; he has the wisdom, compassion, and skill to show us the path. It would be silly to entrust ourselves to a guide who had not reached the enlightened state him or herself.

Our travel guide can give us information about what to take on our trip and what to leave behind. He or she can tell us about changing planes, the various places we'll pass through, what dangers we could encounter along the way, and what resources are available. Similarly, the Buddha described the various levels of the paths and stages, the progression from one to the next, the good qualities to take with us and develop, and the harmful ones to leave behind. However, a travel guide cannot force us to make the journey—he or she can only indicate the way. We have to go to the airport ourselves and get on the plane. Likewise, the Buddha cannot force us to practice the path. He gives the teachings and shows by his example how to do it, but we have to do it ourselves.

The Buddhas as Manifestations

The second way to think of the Buddhas is as manifestations of enlightened minds in the physical forms of various Buddhas and Buddhist deities. Buddhas are omniscient in that they perceive all existent phenomena as clearly as we see the palm of our hand. They achieved this ability by fully developing their wisdom and compassion and thus eliminating all obscurations. But we cannot communicate directly with the Buddhas' omniscient minds because our minds are obscured. For the Buddhas to fulfill their most heartfelt wish to lead all beings to enlightenment, they must communicate with us, and to do so, they assume physical forms. In this way, we can think of Shakyamuni Buddha as a being who was already enlightened, and who appeared in the aspect of a prince in order to teach us.

But if Shakyamuni was already enlightened, how could he take rebirth? He didn't take rebirth under the control of disturbing attitudes and contaminated actions (karma) as ordinary beings do, because he had already eliminated these defilements from his mind. However, he was able to appear on this earth by the power of compassion. Similarly, high-level bodhisattvas—beings who have the constant and intense wish to become Buddhas in order to benefit others—can voluntarily take rebirth, not out of ignorance as ordinary beings do, but out of compassion.

When thinking of the Buddha as a manifestation, we do not emphasize the Buddha as a personality. Rather, we concentrate on the qualities of the omniscient mind appearing in the form of a person. This is a more abstract way of understanding the Buddha, so it takes more effort on our part to think in this way.

In the same way, the various enlightened Buddhist deities can be seen as manifestations of the qualities of omniscient minds. Why are there so many deities if all the beings who have attained enlightenment have the same realizations? Because each physical appearance emphasizes and communicates with different aspects of our personality. This demonstrates the Buddhas' skillful means, their ability to guide each person according to his or her disposition. For example, Avalokiteshvara (Kuan Yin, Chenresig, Kannon) is the manifestation of the compassion of all the Buddhas. Although possessing the same compassion and wisdom of any Buddha, Avalokiteshvara's particular manifestation emphasizes compassion.

Enlightened compassion cannot be seen with the eyes, but if it were to appear in physical form, what would it look like? In the same way that artists express themselves symbolically through images, the Buddhas express their compassion symbolically by appearing in the form of Avalokiteshvara. In some drawings, Avalokiteshvara is white and has a thousand arms. The white color emphasizes purity, in this case the purification of selfishness through compassion. The thousand arms, each with an eye in its palm, express impartial compassion in looking upon all beings and reaching out to help them. Avalokiteshvara's body itself demonstrates compassion. By visualizing compassion in this physical aspect, we can communicate with compassion in a nonverbal and symbolic way.

The deity Manjushri is the manifestation of the wisdom of all the Buddhas. Manjushri has the same realizations as all the Buddhas. In the Tibetan tradition, Manjushri is depicted as golden in color, holding a flaming sword and a lotus flower upon which rests the *Perfection of Wisdom Sutra*. This physical form is symbolic of inner realizations. The golden color represents wisdom, which illuminates the mind just as golden rays of the sun light up the earth. Holding the *Perfection of Wisdom Sutra* indicates that to develop wisdom, we must study, contemplate, and meditate on the meanings contained in this sutra. The sword represents wisdom in its function of cutting through ignorance. By visualizing and meditating on Manjushri, we can attain the qualities of a Buddha, especially wisdom.

These examples help us to understand why there are so many deities. Each emphasizes a particular aspect of the enlightened qualities and communicates that aspect to us symbolically. That does not mean, however, that there is no such being as Avalokiteshvara. On one level, we can understand the Buddha of Compassion to be a person residing in a certain Pure Land—a place where all conditions are conducive for spiritual growth. On another level, we can see Avalokiteshvara as a manifestation of compassion in a physical form. In Tibet, Avalokiteshvara is depicted in a male form and in China in a female form. An enlightened mind is actually beyond being male or female. The various physical forms are simply appearances to communicate with us ordinary beings who are so involved in forms. An enlightened being can appear in a wide variety of bodies. If it is more effective to appear in a female form for people of one culture and a male form for people of another, an enlightened being will do that.

The nature of these various manifestations is the same: the blissful omniscient mind of wisdom and compassion. All of the Buddhas and deities are not separate beings in the same way that an apple and an orange are separate fruits. Rather, they all have the same nature. They only appear in different external forms in order to communicate with us in different ways. From one lump of clay, someone can make a pot, a vase, a plate, or a figurine. The nature of all of them is the same—clay—yet they perform different functions according to how the clay is shaped. In the same way, the nature of all the Buddhas and deities is the blissful omniscient mind of wisdom and compassion. This appears in a variety of forms in order to perform various functions. Thus, when we want to develop compassion, we emphasize meditation on Avalokiteshvara, and when our mind is dull and sluggish, we emphasize the practice of Manjushri, the Buddha of Wisdom. These Buddhas all have the same realizations, yet each one has his or her specialty.

The Buddha That We Will Become

The third way to understand the Buddha is as the appearance of our own Buddha nature in its fully developed form. All beings have the potential to become Buddhas, for all of our minds are innately pure. At the present they are clouded by disturbing attitudes and negative emotions (klesa) and contaminated actions (karma). Through constant practice, we can remove these defilements from our mindstreams and nourish the seeds of the beautiful potentials we have. Thus each of us can become a Buddha when this process of purification and growth is completed. This is a unique feature of Buddhism, for most other religions say an unbridgeable gap exists between the divine being and the human being. However, the Buddha said that each being has the potential to become fully enlightened. It is only a matter of practicing the path and creating the causes to reach enlightenment. Thus there are many beings who have already become Buddhas, and we can become one as well.

When we visualize the Buddha or a deity and think of him or her as the future Buddha that we will become, we are imagining our now latent Buddha nature in its completely developed form. We are thinking of the future, when we will have completed the path to enlightenment. By imagining the future in the present, we reaffirm our own latent goodness. The future Buddha we will become is the real protection from our suffering, because by becoming this Buddha, we will have eliminated the causes for our present unsatisfactory conditions.

These different ways of understanding the Buddha are progressively more difficult to understand. We may not grasp them immediately. That's all right. Various interpretations are explained because people have different ways of understanding. We aren't expected to all think in the same way or to understand everything at once.

If there are people alive today who have attained Buddhahood, why don't they tell us who they are and demonstrate their clairvoyant powers to generate faith in others? Why do the great masters all deny having spiritual realizations?

One of the principal qualities of an enlightened being is humility. It would be out of character for Buddhas to boast about their attainments and to egotistically gather disciples. By their genuine respect for all beings and their willingness to learn from everyone, great spiritual masters set a good example for us. We ordinary beings tend to show off our qualities and even brag about talents and achievements that we do not have. Advanced practitioners are the opposite: they remain humble.

The Buddha forbade his followers to display their clairvoyant or miraculous powers unless circumstances deemed it absolutely necessary, and they were not allowed to talk about them. There are several reasons for this. If one has clairvoyant powers and displays them, one's pride could increase and this would be detrimental to one's practice. Also, others might get superstitious and think that clairvoyant powers are the goal of the path. In fact, they are a side effect and are useful only if one has the proper motivation of impartial loving-kindness for all. In addition, if a Buddha, with a body made of radiant light, suddenly appeared on the street, people would be so shocked that they couldn't pay attention to that Buddha's teachings. It is more skillful for those who have attained high levels of the path to appear in ordinary form. We may notice that they have exceptional qualities, but the fact that they look just like us allows us to feel closer to them. It gives us the confidence that we too can develop the same enlightened qualities that they have.

What does "faith" mean in Buddhism? Can we receive grace from the Buddhas?

Buddhism encourages us to learn the Buddha's teachings and to try them out, and in that way develop faith, confidence, and trust in them. Buddhism speaks of three types of confidence:

1) Pure or admiring confidence. We admire the qualities of the Buddha, Dharma, and Sangha by knowing their qualities.
2) Aspiring confidence. By recognizing the qualities of the Three Jewels, we aspire to become like them.
3) Confidence from conviction. By examining the teachings and applying them in our lives, we develop the conviction that they are effective.

Buddhism does not use the word "grace" per se, but there is a similar concept, which is translated as receiving the inspiration or the blessings of the Three Jewels. This means that our minds are transformed as a result not only of the influence of the Three Jewels, but also of our practice and openness.

Chapter Three

LOVE AND COMPASSION

From a Buddhist view, what are love and compassion? Why are they important?

Love is the wish for all sentient beings (any being with a mind who is not yet fully enlightened) to have happiness and its causes. Compassion is the wish for them to be free of suffering and its causes. We work over time to cultivate these feelings towards all beings equally—ourselves, those we know and those we don't.

Love and compassion benefit ourselves and others. With them, we feel in touch with and connect to all living beings. Feelings of alienation and despair vanish and are replaced with optimism. When we act with such feelings, those in our immediate environment benefit from being near a kind person. Our family feels the difference, as do our colleagues, friends, and people we encounter during the day. Developing love and compassion is one way we can contribute to world peace. In addition it leaves many good imprints on our mindstream so that our spiritual practice progresses better and we become more receptive to realizing the path to enlightenment.

Buddhism talks about loving all beings impartially. Is this possible?

Yes, it is. This involves looking beyond superficial appearances into others' hearts and recognizing that each sentient being wants to be happy and to avoid suffering as intensely as we do. In this way, all sentient beings are equal. Continually familiarizing our mind with this view deflates the judgmental, critical mind that loves to pick out faults in others. For example, when we are waiting in a line, we comment to ourselves about the people around us, "This one is too thin. Why does this one dress like that? This person looks aggressive. That one is showing off." Such self-talk is based on superficial appearances and false assumptions, and it only serves to reinforce prejudice and make us feel alienated from others. If we train our mind to look deeper and to recognize that each person is just like us in wanting happiness and not wanting pain, then we will feel a common bond with everyone and will be able to wish everyone well equally. Needless to say, such an attitude must be cultivated over time. We cannot simply think this a few times and expect all our biases to instantly disappear!

We are creatures of habit and need to put effort into pulling ourselves out of habitual judgments, emotional responses, and behaviors towards others. Each moment of our life is a new one with the opportunity to experiment and do things differently. Each time we meet someone we have an opportunity to connect, to give and exchange kindness. If only we would wake up and take advantage of each opportunity, for so many exist each day!

If we love everyone equally, wouldn't normal social relationships break down?

Love is an emotion in our heart that we want to cultivate towards everyone. But that does not mean we treat everyone in exactly the same way. For example, we still recognize children's limitations and abilities and relate to them as children, not as adults. Clearly, we treat people we know differently than those we don't because conventional socially accepted roles still hold. If someone is upset with us, we must listen, communicate, and try to resolve the conflict. We don't treat them as if no conflict existed, as that would make them feel we weren't hearing them. Nevertheless, no matter what type of relationship we have with a particular person at a certain moment, we can still care for everyone equally in our hearts.

What is the difference between compassion and pity?

Compassion is the wish for all sentient beings to be free from suffering and its causes. Like love, this is generated on the basis of seeing everyone's happiness and suffering as equally significant. Whereas there is a power differential in the case of pity, none exists when we have compassion. With pity, we see ourselves as being superior and with condescension and false care, have pity on those who we consider inferior to us. Compassion, on the other hand, is very direct and equal. Suffering is to be removed no matter whose it is, and if we have the opportunity to help in a small or large way, we will.

For example, when we step on a thorn, our hand reaches down, pulls it out, and bandages the foot. The hand doesn't say, "Foot, you're so stupid! I told you to watch where you're going, but you didn't. Now I have to fix you up. Don't forget that you owe me a favor!" Why doesn't the hand "think" like this? Because the hand and the foot are part of the same organism, and they help each other naturally and without thinking. Similarly, if we consider ourselves part of the same organism of all sentient life, we will reach out to others as if they were us. That is the type of compassion we try to develop through practice.

What about loving ourselves and having compassion for ourselves?

Caring for ourselves is important. Buddhism doesn't talk about neglecting ourselves in the name of compassion so that we become a burden on others and they have to take care of us. Rather, we have to love and take care of ourselves in a healthy way, not an obsessive way. We must keep our body clean and take care of our health. We must keep a happy attitude, so that we can, in turn, give to others with good will and cheerfulness. Loving and having compassion for ourselves doesn't mean indulging our every wish or holding ourselves first. If we care about every small thing that happens to us and make a big deal about every emotion we feel, we will become too sensitive and too easily offended. This will make us more miserable. Self-obsession and self-love are very different.

His Holiness the Dalai Lama says, "If you want to be selfish, be wisely selfish. Care for others!" If we are self-centered and ignore others' concerns or place them second to our own, others will be unhappy. We, then, will live in an unhappy environment, which will impede our own happiness. If we care for others, they are happy and then where we live has a good feeling, which in turn helps us to be happy. In addition, actions motivated by self-preoccupation plant negative karmic seeds on our mindstreams, ripening in unpleasant experiences for us, while actions motivated by genuine care and concern for others create good karmic seeds, which will bring about happiness for ourselves.

The determination to be free from cyclic existence and to attain nirvana, which is the first of the three principal aspects of the path (the others being the altruistic intention and the wisdom realizing emptiness), means having compassion for ourselves. Not wanting to continue suffering in cyclic existence, we develop the aspiration to be free from it. That type of compassion for ourselves is necessary for our own spiritual progress. It also is a prerequisite for generating compassion for all other sentient beings.

What is the difference between being attached to other people and loving them? Why is attachment problematic?

In Buddhism, attachment is defined as an attitude that exaggerates other people's good qualities or projects good qualities that aren't there and then clings to these people. With attachment, we care for others because they please us. They give us presents, praise us, help, and encourage us. With love, we want sentient beings to have happiness and its causes simply because they are living beings just like ourselves. When we are attached to others, we don't see them for who they are and thereby develop many expectations of them, thinking they should be like this and they should do that. Then, when they don't live up to what we thought they were or should be, we feel hurt, disillusioned, and angry.

When we love others, we don't expect anything in return. We accept people for who they are and try to help them, but we aren't concerned with how we'll benefit from the relationship. Real love isn't jealous, possessive or limited to just a few near and dear ones. Rather, it's impartial and is felt for all beings.

If we stop expecting things from others and give up our attachment to them, isn't there danger of becoming cynical and losing trust in people?

As a society we expect certain manners and behavior from others according to the situation. For example, we expect to be greeted by our co-worker when we greet him or her. We expect the people with whom we are working on a project to do their share. Such expectations are normal. The difficulty sets in when we get angry or hurt when someone doesn't fulfill our expectations. We may think, "Okay, I just won't expect anything from anyone," but such an attitude is cynicism, which is just another negative emotion and should not be confused with giving up attachment. The attitude we want to develop still hopes that others will be reliable, but does not expect them always to be so. We still have a basic trust in people being kind, but we can accept it when they aren't, for we remember that they, just like us, are sometimes overwhelmed by negative emotions or confusion.

If we're detached, is it possible to be with our friends and family?

"Detachment" isn't an accurate translation of the Buddhist concept. "Non-attachment" may be better. Detachment implies being uninvolved, cold, and aloof. However, in the Buddhist sense, non-attachment means having a balanced attitude, free from clinging. When we are free from attachment, we won't have unrealistic expectations of others, nor will we cling to them out of fear of being miserable when they aren't there. Non-attachment is a calm, realistic, open, and accepting attitude. It isn't hostile, paranoid, or unsociable. Having a balanced attitude doesn't mean rejecting our friends and family. It means relating to them in a different way. When we aren't attached, our relationships with others are harmonious, and in fact, our affection for them increases.

Buddhism emphasizes cherishing others before self. Can this lead to codependent relationships in which one person constantly sacrifices his or her own needs in order to please the other?

No, not if it is properly understood. Taking care of others can be done with two very different motivations. With one, we care for others in an unhealthy way, seemingly sacrificing ourselves, but really acting out of fear or attachment. People who are attached to praise, reputation, relationships, and so forth and who fear losing these may seemingly neglect their own needs to take care of others. But in fact, they are protecting themselves in an unproductive way. Their care comes not from genuine love, but from a self-centered attempt to be happy that is actually making them more unhappy.

The other way of taking care of others is motivated by genuine affection, and this is what the Buddha encouraged. This kind of affection and respect for others doesn't seek or expect something in return. It is rooted in the knowledge that all other beings want to be happy and to avoid pain just as much as we do. In addition, they have all helped us either in previous lives or in this present life by doing whatever job they do in society. By steeping our minds in such thoughts, we'll naturally feel affection for others and our motivation to help them will be based on genuinely wanting them to be happy.

Codependence doesn't arise from one person in a relationship being manipulative, dependent, or demanding. It evolves when two or more people's attachment, anger, and fear mutually feed into each other's in unhealthy ways. If one person has cultivated non-attachment and acts with genuine love and compassion, even if the other consciously or unconsciously tries to manipulate him or her, the person with a clear motivation won't get hooked into a pattern of unhealthy interactions.

Chapter Four

MEDITATION

What is meditation?

Nowadays meditation is sometimes confused with other activities. Meditation is not simply relaxing the body and mind. Nor is it imagining being a successful person with wonderful possessions, good relationships, appreciation from others, and fame. This is merely daydreaming about objects of attachment. Meditation is not sitting in the full vajra position, with an arrow-straight back and a holy expression on our face. Meditation is a mental activity. Even if the body is in perfect position, if our mind is running wild thinking about objects of attachment or anger, we're not meditating. Meditation is also not a concentrated state, such as we may have when painting, reading, or doing any activity that interests us. Nor is it simply being aware of what we are doing at any particular moment.

The Tibetan word for meditation is *gom*. This has the same verbal root as "to habituate" or "to familiarize." Meditation means habituating ourselves to constructive, realistic, and beneficial emotions and attitudes. It builds up good habits of the mind. Meditation is used to transform our thoughts and views so that they are more compassionate and correspond to reality.

How do we learn to meditate? What kinds of meditation are there?

These days many people teach meditation and spiritual paths, but we should examine them well and not just excitedly jump into something. Some people think that they can invent their own way to meditate and don't need to learn from a skilled teacher. This is very unwise. If we wish to meditate, we must first receive instruction from a qualified teacher. Listening to teachings given by a reliable source like the Buddha is to our advantage, because these teachings have been studied by scholars and practiced by skilled meditators who have attained results throughout the centuries. In this way, we can establish that the lineage of teachings and meditation practice is valid and worthy of being practiced. Such a practice was not merely concocted according to someone's whim.

First, we listen to teachings and deepen our understanding by thinking about them. Then, through meditation we integrate what we have learned with our mind. For example, we hear teachings on how to develop impartial love for all beings. Next, we check up and investigate whether that is possible. We come to understand each step in the practice. Then, we build up this good habit of the mind by integrating it with our being and training ourselves in the various steps leading to the experience of impartial love. That is meditation.

Meditation is of two general types: stabilizing and analytical. The former is designed to develop concentration and the latter to develop understanding and insight. Within these two broad categories, the Buddha taught a wide variety of meditation techniques, and the lineages of these are extant today. An example of stabilizing meditation is focusing our mind on our breath and observing all the sensations that occur as we breathe. This calms our mind and frees it from its usual chatter, enabling us to be more peaceful in our daily life and not to worry so much. The visualized image of the Buddha may also be used as the object upon which we stabilize our mind and develop concentration. While some non-Buddhist traditions suggest looking at a flower or candle to develop concentration, this is generally not recommended by Buddhist traditions because meditation is an activity of our mental consciousness, not our sense consciousness.

Other meditations help us to control anger, attachment, and jealousy by developing positive and realistic attitudes toward other people. These are instances of analytical or "checking" meditation. Other examples are reflecting on our precious human life, impermanence, and the emptiness of inherent existence. Here we practice thinking in constructive ways in order to gain proper understanding and eventually go beyond conceptual thought.

Purification meditations cleanse the imprints of negative actions and stop nagging feelings of guilt. Meditating on a koan—a perplexing puzzle designed to break our usual fixed conceptions—is done in some Zen (Ch'an) traditions. Some meditations involve visualization and mantra recitation. These are a few of the many types of meditation taught in Buddhism.

What are the benefits of meditation?

By building up good habits of the mind in meditation, our behavior in daily life gradually changes. Our anger decreases, we are better able to make decisions, and we become less dissatisfied and restless. These results of meditation can be experienced now. But we should always try to have a broader and more encompassing motivation to meditate than just our own present happiness. If we generate the motivation to meditate in order to make preparation for future lives, to attain liberation from the cycle of constantly recurring problems, or to reach the state of full enlightenment for the benefit of all beings, then naturally our minds will also be peaceful now. In addition, we'll be able to attain those high and noble goals.

Having a regular meditation practice—even if it's only for a short time each day—is extremely beneficial. Some people think, "My day is so busy with career, family, and social obligations that I cannot meditate. I'll leave it until I'm older and my life is less busy. Daily meditation is the job of monks and nuns." This is incorrect! If meditation is helpful to us, we should make time for it every day. Even if we don't want to meditate, having some "quiet time" for ourselves each day is important. We need time to sit peacefully and reflect upon what we do and why, to read a Dharma book, or to do some chanting. To be happy, we must learn to like our own company and to be content alone. Setting aside some quiet time, preferably in the morning before the start of the day's activities, is necessary, especially in modern societies where people are so busy.

We always have time to nourish our bodies. We seldom skip meals because we see they are important. Likewise, we should reserve time to nourish our mind and heart, because they too are important for our sense of well-being. After all, it is our mind, not our body, that continues on to future lives, carrying with it the karmic imprints of our actions. Dharma practice is not done for the Buddha's benefit, but for our own. The Dharma describes how to create the causes for happiness, and since we all want happiness, we should practice the Dharma as much as we can.

Some Buddhist traditions use visualization and mantra recitation during meditation while others discourage these. Why?

The Buddha taught a variety of techniques because different people have different inclinations. Each technique may approach a similar goal but from a different vantage point. For example, when doing breathing meditation, emphasis is placed on developing concentration on the breath itself. In this case, visualizing something would distract us from the object of meditation, which is the breath.

However, another meditation technique uses the visualized image of the Buddha as its object of meditation. A purification meditation could involve, for example, visualization of the Buddha with light radiating from the Buddha into us and all the beings who we imagine seated around us. This meditation takes the natural tendency of our mind to imagine things and transforms it into the path to enlightenment. Instead of imagining a holiday with our boyfriend or girlfriend, which just incites our attachment, we imagine the serene figure of the Buddha, which inspires a balanced and peaceful state of mind.

Similarly, reciting mantras takes the natural tendency of our mind to chatter and transforms it into the path. Rather than continuing our internal dialogue about what we like and what we don't, we use that inner voice to recite mantras. Mantra recitation helps us to develop concentration and can have a purifying effect on the mind.

Is it better to do just one type of meditation or a variety?

This depends on the specific Buddhist tradition we follow and on the instructions of our spiritual teacher. Those in the Tibetan Buddhist tradition train in several different types of meditation because many different aspects of our character need to be cultivated. Thus, we may do breathing meditation to calm the mind, loving-kindness meditation to generate compassion and altruism for others, visualization of the Buddha or a deity along with mantra recitation to purify negative karmic imprints, and analytical meditation combined with concentration to develop the wisdom realizing emptiness. When we have developed a general overall view of the gradual path to enlightenment, we'll understand the purpose of each meditation and where it fits in along the path. Then we can gradually develop many different abilities and sides of our character.

Can one develop clairvoyant powers through practicing Buddhism? Is this a worthwhile goal to pursue?

Yes, one can, but that isn't the principal goal of Dharma practice. Some people get very excited about the prospect of having clairvoyance. "Wait until I tell my friends about this! Everyone will think I'm special and will come to ask me for advice." What an egotistical motivation for wanting to be clairvoyant! If we still get angry and are unable to control what we say, think, and do, what use is running after clairvoyance? Desiring clairvoyant powers because we want to be famous and well-respected is not only a distraction to our practice, but antithetical to it. Becoming a kind and altruistic person benefits both ourselves and others much more.

Once a child asked me if I had clairvoyance. Could I bend a spoon through concentration? Could I stop a clock or walk through a wall? I told him no, and even if I could, what use would it be? Would that lessen the suffering in the world? In fact, the person whose spoon I ruined may suffer more! The point of our human existence isn't to build up our egos, but to develop a kind heart and a sense of universal responsibility working for world peace. Loving-kindness is the real miracle!

If one has a kind heart, then developing clairvoyant powers could be beneficial for others. However, sincere practitioners do not go around advertising their clairvoyance. In fact, most of them will deny they have such abilities and will be very humble. The Buddha warned against public displays of clairvoyance unless they were necessary to benefit others. Humble people are actually more impressive than boastful ones. Their serenity and respect for others shine through, and this gladdens our heart. People who have subdued pride, have loving-kindness toward others, and are developing their wisdom are people we can trust. Such people are working for the benefit of others, not for their own prestige and wealth.

Can meditation be dangerous? Some people say you can go crazy from it. Is that true?

If we learn to meditate from an experienced teacher who instructs us in a reliable method, and if we follow these instructions correctly, there is no danger at all. Meditation is simply building up good habits of the mind. We do this in a gradual fashion. Thus, doing advanced practices without proper instruction is unwise. If we build up our capabilities gradually, we will be able to progress to more advanced practices without difficulty, and one day will become a Buddha.

Chapter Five

IMPERMANENCE AND SUFFERING

Buddhism talks a lot about impermanence, death and suffering. Isn't such an approach to life unhealthy and pessimistic?

The word "suffering" is not an accurate translation of the Pali or Sanskrit word *dukha*. Dukha has the connotation of unsatisfactory experiences. It means that everything isn't completely wonderful in our lives. While most of us don't feel we are suffering all the time, we would agree that not everything in our lives is perfect. Even when we're relatively happy, there's no guarantee that things will continue to go well. One small event can change our entire experience. This is what is meant by unsatisfactory experiences, dukha, or suffering. The Buddha merely described our present situation. Therefore he was being realistic, not pessimistic. His motivation for describing this was to help us seek the means to free ourselves from it.

The purpose of contemplating impermanence, death, and unsatisfactory experiences isn't to become depressed and have the joy taken out of life. Rather, the purpose is to rid ourselves of attachment and false expectations. If we become emotionally afraid or depressed when thinking about these things, then we are not contemplating them correctly. Meditating on these subjects should make our minds calm and lucid because it decreases our clinging attachment and the confusion that attachment causes in our lives.

At present, our minds are easily overwhelmed by the false projections of attachment. We see people and objects in an unrealistic way. Things are changing moment by moment but they appear to us to be constant and unchanging. That is why we are upset when they break. We may say, "All these things are impermanent," but our words aren't consistent with our innate view, which mistakenly considers our body and our loved ones to be unchanging. This unrealistic conception causes us pain, because we have expectations of things and people that cannot be fulfilled. Our loved ones cannot live forever; a relationship doesn't remain the same; the new car will not always be the shiny model just off the showroom floor. Thus, we are perpetually disappointed when we must part with the people we care for, when our possessions break, when our body becomes weak or old. If we had a more realistic view of these things and accepted their impermanence—not just with our words but with our heart—then such disappointment would not come.

Contemplating impermanence and death also eliminates many of the useless worries that prevent us from being happy and relaxed. Ordinarily, we become upset when we are criticized or insulted. We are angry when our possessions are stolen and feel jealous if someone else gets the promotion we wanted. We are proud of our looks or athletic ability. All of these attitudes are disturbing emotions that leave harmful imprints on our mindstream and bring us problems in our future lives as well as in this life. However, if we contemplate the transient nature of these things, we accept that our life will end and that none of these things can accompany us at death. Understanding that, we will stop exaggerating their importance, and they will no longer be so problematic for us.

That doesn't mean that we become apathetic towards the people and environment around us. On the contrary, by eliminating the wrong conception of permanence and the disturbing attitudes that stem from it, our minds will become clearer and we'll be able to enjoy things for what they are. We'll live more in the present, appreciating things as they are now, without fantasies about what they should be or might become. We'll worry less about small matters and will be less distracted when we meditate. We will not be so touchy about how others treat us. By reflecting on impermanence and unsatisfactory experiences, we can deal better with all the unpleasant events that occur because we are still in the cycle of constantly recurring problems. In short, by correctly contemplating these truths, our mental state will become healthier.

Thus the understanding of our mortality inspires us to think deeply about what is important in life and to set clear priorities. If we do so, our life will be more vibrant and when the time of death arrives, we will have no regrets. For example, no one dies thinking, "I should have worked more overtime." But people do die regretting that they mistreated others or did not tell those they loved that they loved them. People die regretting that they did minimal spiritual practice. By reflecting on death in advance, we will do what is important while we are alive and will avoid such regrets at the time of death.

Why is there suffering? How can we stop it?

Unsatisfactory experiences occur simply because the causes for them exist. One cause is our disturbing attitudes, such as ignorance, attachment, and anger. The other is the harmful actions we have engaged in, such as killing, stealing, and lying, which are motivated by disturbing attitudes. By developing the wisdom realizing selflessness, we will eliminate the disturbing attitudes and the contaminated actions they cause, thus stopping the source of our problems. As a result, the painful consequences will not follow, and instead, we'll abide in nirvana, a state of lasting happiness. In the meantime, before we generate this wisdom, by doing purification practices we will impede the ripening of the results of our previous destructive actions. The Buddha also taught many techniques for mentally transforming difficult circumstances into the path to enlightenment. We can learn about these and practice them when we have problems.

Do we have to suffer to attain liberation (nirvana)? Must we renounce the world to become a Buddha?

Practicing Buddha's teachings brings happiness, not pain. The spiritual path itself isn't painful, and there is no special virtue in suffering. We already have enough problems, so there's no sense in causing ourselves more in the name of practicing religion. However, that doesn't mean that we won't have any problems while practicing the Dharma. While we're on the path, previous destructive actions that haven't yet been purified may ripen and bring problems. When this happens, we can transform the situation into the path to enlightenment by using the various techniques the Buddha taught. Sometimes our anger, attachment, or jealousy may arise strongly and be very disquieting when we're trying to practice. This happens because our disturbing attitudes haven't yet been eliminated. After all, we don't become Buddhas after practicing the Dharma for just a short time! We can apply the Buddha's teachings to subdue these unpleasant emotions while being patient with ourselves and recognizing that purifying our minds takes time.

Although the English word "renunciation" is often used in Buddhist translations, it doesn't convey the precise meaning. It is more accurate to say that we must develop the determination to be free from cyclic existence and to attain liberation. We don't need to renounce people and things. Rather, we need to give up our clinging attachment to them. There is nothing inherently wrong with the world; the real problem lies in our disturbing attitudes. For example, money isn't the problem; it is merely sheets of paper. However, our clinging to and craving for money cause big problems. These erroneous and harmful attitudes are to be given up. Of course, if we are very attached to something, it's a good idea to distance ourselves from it for a while to calm our clinging. If we're attached to ice cream, it's better not to go to an ice cream parlor! Later, when we've developed a more balanced and altruistic motivation, we can actually use the objects of our previous attachment to benefit others.

Buddhism talks about accepting our suffering and also about freeing ourselves from suffering. Are these contradictory?

No. Accepting our difficulties doesn't mean becoming apathetic and resigned to suffering. Rather, our experience at a particular moment—whatever it is—is the reality of that moment. When we refuse to accept this, we find ourselves in conflict with reality. On the other hand, we can accept our present unhappiness and still work to free ourselves from future unsatisfactory experiences. For example, if we accept the transient nature of our world, we will cease trying to control things that, by their nature, are out of our control. We will be at peace with whatever life presents and simultaneously work to benefit others with an altruistic aspiration that appreciates every being's potential to transcend suffering and become enlightened.

Chapter Six

SELFLESSNESS

Do "selflessness" and "emptiness" have the same meaning? What is the advantage of realizing selflessness or emptiness?

In general, these two terms are synonymous, although when studying philosophy in depth, there are differences between them. By realizing emptiness, we will be able to cleanse our minds of all defilements and obscurations. At the moment, our minds are obscured by ignorance: the way we perceive ourselves and other phenomena as existing is not the way that they really exist. It's similar to people who wear sunglasses all the time. Everything they see appears dark, and they think that is the way things are. In fact, if they took their sunglasses off, they would find that things actually exist in a different way.

Another analogy for the view of ignorance is an audience who watches a movie and thinks that the people on the screen are real. The viewers become very emotional and involved in the fate of the characters. Being attached to the hero, they are antagonistic towards the characters who threaten him. The audience may even cry out, cringe, or jump up in their seat when the hero is harmed. In fact, these reactions are out of proportion, for there are no real people on the screen at all. They are only projections, which are dependent on causes and conditions such as the film, the film projector, and the screen. Realizing emptiness is analogous to understanding that the movie is empty of real people. However, the appearance of the characters does exist, dependent on the film, actors, screen, and so forth.

If we understand this, we can still enjoy the film, but no longer go up and down emotionally as the hero experiences various events.

By generating the wisdom that directly realizes emptiness, we will perceive the mode in which we and other phenomena exist: they are empty of our fantasized projections on them, most importantly the projection of inherent existence. Having this wisdom realizing reality, we'll gradually free ourselves from the bonds of the ignorance that misconceives reality. Familiarizing our minds with emptiness, we'll gradually eliminate all ignorance, anger, attachment, pride, jealousy, and other disturbing attitudes and negative emotions from our mindstream. By doing so, we'll cease to engage in the destructive actions motivated by them. Freed from the influence of ignorance, negative emotions, and the actions motivated by them, we'll be liberated from the causes of our problems, and thus the problems also will cease. In other words, the wisdom realizing emptiness is the true path to happiness.

What does it mean to say, "All persons and phenomena are empty of true or inherent existence?"

This means that persons (like you and me) and all other phenomena (tables, etc.) are empty of these fantasized qualities that we project onto them. One of the principal deceptive qualities that we project onto persons and phenomena is that they are inherently existent, that is, that they exist without depending on causes and conditions, parts, and the consciousness which conceives them and gives them a name. Thus, in our ordinary view, things appear to have some true or inherent nature, as if they were really there, as if we could find these real, independent entities if we searched for them. They appear to be there, independent of the causes and conditions that created them, independent of the parts of which they are made, and independent of the mind which conceives and labels them. This is the appearance of true or inherent existence, and our minds grasp it as real.

However, when we examine things analytically to discover if things exist in the independent way they superficially appear to, we find that they do not. They are empty of these fantasized projections.

Still, they do exist, but they exist dependently, for they rely on causes and conditions, on the parts which compose them, and on the mind which conceives them and gives them a name.

If all people and phenomena are selfless or empty, does that mean that nothing exists?

No, phenomena and people still exist. After all, I am still here typing and you are still reading! Emptiness is not the same as nihilism. Rather, people and phenomena are empty of our fantasized projections upon them. They lack what our wrong conceptions attribute to them. They do not exist in the way they appear to us at present, but they do exist. That is, they don't exist independently, but they do dependently exist. For example, someone wearing sunglasses sees dark trees. There are no *independent* dark trees, but we cannot say there are no trees at all. The trees exist: they just do not exist in the way they appear to the person with sunglasses.

Is realizing emptiness the same as having a blank mind, free from all thoughts?

No. When emptiness is directly realized, the mind is free from thoughts and concepts. However, just removing all thoughts from our mind—peaceful though it may be—is not the realization of emptiness. After all, cows' minds are pretty blank—they do not have many conceptual thoughts—but they haven't realized emptiness! Realizing emptiness involves first understanding what things are empty of—inherent existence—and then realizing that inherent existence is a hallucination that has never existed at all.

Sometimes people feel that their lives are empty. Is this the same emptiness spoken of by the Buddha?

No. In everyday language, we say people feel empty when they lack goals or close relationships with others or lack a sense of meaning in their lives. This is a lack of external relationships, clear personal goals, or internal tranquility. It is resolved by developing self-confidence, setting priorities in life, and letting go of unrealistic expectations.

The emptiness that the Buddha spoke of, on the other hand, concerns the mode of existence of phenomena. It is the absence of inherent existence. That is, things do not exist under their own power, from their own side, independent of all other things. Understanding this emptiness leads to a feeling of fullness and meaning in our lives because we will be free from all restricting misconceptions and disturbing emotions. This emptiness is realized through studying, thinking about, and meditating on the Buddha's teachings.

Psychologists tell us that a strong sense of self is essential to be psychologically healthy. But it seems Buddhism says there is no self. How can we reconcile these two views?

When psychologists speak of a sense of "self" they are referring to the feeling that oneself is an efficacious person, someone who is self-confident and can act in the world. Buddhists agree that such a sense of self is both realistic and necessary. However, the sense of self that Buddhism says is unrealistic is that of a very solid, unchanging, independent "I." Such a self never has and never will exist. To understand this is to realize emptiness.

Strange though it may sound, someone may have a psychologically weak sense of self that in Buddhist parlance would be considered strong self-grasping. For example, a person with poor self-esteem may focus a lot on himself and have a strong feeling of the existence of an independent self that is inferior, unlovable, and a failure. From a Buddhist viewpoint, such a independent self does not exist, although a conventional self does.

What is the best way to realize the emptiness of inherent existence?

This realization is difficult to gain and is attained at advanced stages of the path, so we must develop our understanding slowly. The path to liberation and enlightenment is a gradual one that is practiced in steps. First we train in the elementary aspects of the path, such as impermanence, refuge, the determination to be free from cyclic existence, love, and compassion. Then we listen to teachings on emptiness from knowledgeable and compassionate spiritual masters. As we think about and discuss these teachings, our understanding will become clearer. Once we have a clear idea of the subject, we can begin to integrate it into our mind through meditation.

One meditation on emptiness of the person is called the four point analysis. The first point is to identify the negated object, that is, the inherently existent thing that does not exist. To do this we recall a time when we had a strong negative emotion, for example, when someone unfairly accused us and there was a strong sense of an independent "I." The second point is to determine that if such an independent "I" existed, it would have to be either totally the same as either the body or mind or completely unrelated to the body and mind. Then, keeping one part of our attention focused on the sense of that independent "I" , we investigate to discover if we can find it. We examine our body to see if any part of our body is our self. We examine our mind to see if any mental state or consciousness is our self. That is the third point. In the fourth point, we investigate if the self is somewhere else, totally separate from the body and mind. Determining that such an independent self cannot be found anywhere, we then conclude that it does not exist at all. That absence of an inherently existent self is the emptiness of the person. We then focus on that single-pointedly.

In doing the meditation on emptiness, we must be careful not to fall to the extreme of nihilism, thinking that no self at all exists. While an independent self does not exist, a conventional, dependent one does.

Chapter Seven

SCIENCE, CREATION, AND REBIRTH

What is the relationship between Buddhism and science?

They have many points in common: for example, both depend on logic and investigation to ascertain the nature of phenomena. Both discourage blind faith and encourage free inquiry on the part of the student. Buddhism does not contradict current scientific theories about the origin of this universe or the physical evolution of the human species. In fact, His Holiness the Dalai Lama has said that if scientific findings contradict what is written in Buddhist scriptures, then Buddhists must accept that new information. However, if science cannot actively disprove what is stated in the scriptures, there is no need to abandon that concept. For example, although scientists have not yet proven the existence of rebirth, they have not been able to disprove it.

Both science and Buddhism use the theory of cause and effect to explain how things function. Science investigates cause and effect as it functions in the physical, material world, whereas Buddhism explores it in terms of the mind.

Both emphasize the dependent nature of phenomena. Things rely on causes, the parts of which they are composed, and the consciousness that observes and labels them. Quantum physicists are becoming increasingly aware of the latter when doing experiments. They recognize that the experimenter is not an independent entity who objectively observes external phenomena. Rather, he or she influences the results of an experiment simply by observing it. This relates to the Buddha's teaching on the emptiness of inherent existence, which emphasizes the dependent relationship between consciousness and the objects it perceives.

Many scientists believe it is impossible to find the smallest partless particles from which all matter is created. Buddhism agrees that isolating these smallest independent particles is impossible. Yet at meetings with scientists, His Holiness the Dalai Lama has mentioned a dependently existing "space particle," which contains the potentials of all other elements in the universe. What precisely is meant by "space particle" and how it relates to scientific theories and discoveries needs to be explored further.

The Buddhist concept of dependent arising can also be applied in the area of neurology, where perception is seen not as an isolated phenomenon, but as the coming together of various factors. Just as scientists say it is impossible to set apart one particular cell or chemical-electrical process that constitutes perception, so Buddhists say that cognition is dependent on a variety of factors, none of which constitutes perception in and of itself.

More scientists are becoming interested in Buddhism, and some Buddhist scholars are learning about modern science. His Holiness the Dalai Lama has attended several conferences with scientists that have been fruitful for everyone concerned. In addition, he encourages monks and nuns to learn about science and to incorporate scientific views into the debates they hold.

How was the world created?

Everything that is created arises from the causes that produce it. Something cannot be created out of nothing. The physical world of forms that we see around us was produced by previous moments of form. This is the field investigated by scientists. At present, many scientists agree on the "big bang" theory, in which all forms of our universe were once tightly condensed. But even the matter that existed before the big bang had causes. It was a continuation of subtler physical elements that, in turn, were a continuation from universes that existed before ours. In this way, the continuity of form is traced back infinitely.

What is the mind?

Our mind is all of our emotional and cognitive experiences. It includes not only the consciousnesses that perceive sense objects—colors and shapes, sounds, odors, tastes, and tactile objects—but also the mental consciousness, which thinks and which has the capacity to directly perceive more subtle objects, such as emptiness. The word "mind" in a Buddhist sense also includes what in English is referred to as "heart," as in "he has a kind heart." To emphasize the continuity of consciousness, we also use the word "mindstream" to refer to our mind. Each person has a separate mind, or mindstream. The mind is formless, while the brain is part of the body. Our body and our mind are separate entities. While the mind is immaterial, the body is material, composed of atoms.

What is the relationship between the brain and the mind?

The brain is a physical organ and is atomic in nature. The mind is formless and is characterized by clarity and awareness. While we're alive, our brain and mind influence each other. The brain provides the physical support for our sense consciousnesses and gross mental consciousness. If the brain and central nervous system are damaged, the functioning of the mind is affected. Similarly, our mental state—be it peaceful or agitated—affects our physical health and our nervous system.

There are subtler levels of mind that, according to Buddhism, do not rely on the physical body as a support. The subtlest mind, which continues on to the next life, is an example. Thus, skilled practitioners can meditate with their subtlest consciousness even after they are brain-dead. Kyabje Ling Rinpoche, His Holiness the Dalai Lama's senior tutor, did this for thirteen days after his breath ceased. Scientists are very interested in studying this, and His Holiness the Dalai Lama has given his approval for them to measure great practitioners' brain functions at death and afterward. The problem is that scheduling this is difficult, because the scientists must be ready with their equipment in India when a great practitioner dies!

What is rebirth?

Rebirth refers to a person's mind taking one body after another under the power of ignorance and contaminated actions. While we are alive, our body and mind are linked, but at death they separate. Each has its own continuum. The body becomes a corpse, and the mind continues on to take another body.

This process of rebirth under the control of ignorance and contaminated actions is cyclic existence, the cycle of constantly recurring problems that we experience. In cyclic existence, sentient beings take rebirth in any of six types of life forms. Some of these life forms—hellish ones, hungry ghosts, and animals—experience more suffering than happiness. Other life forms—humans, demi-gods, and gods—are considered relatively happy births. Beings repeatedly take rebirth in all of these life forms until they free themselves from ignorance and attain liberation.

How did our mind begin? Who or what created it?

Each moment of mind is a continuation of the previous moment. Who we are and what we think and feel depends on who we were yesterday. Our present mind is a continuation of yesterday's mind. That is why we can remember what happened to us in the past. One moment of our mind was caused by the previous moment of mind. This continuity can be traced back to childhood and to being a fetus in our mother's womb. Even before the time of conception, our mindstream existed. Its previous moments were linked to another body.

Our mind has no beginning, and its continuity is infinite. This may be difficult to grasp initially, but if we use the example of a number line, it becomes easier. From the "0" position, looking left, there is no first negative number, and looking right, there is no last, highest number. One more can always be added. In the same way, our mindstream has no beginning and no end. We all have had an infinite number of past rebirths, and our mind will continue to exist infinitely.

In fact, it would be impossible for our mindstream to have a beginning. Because each moment of mind is caused by its previous moment, if a beginning existed, then either the first moment of mind had no cause or it was caused by something other than a previous moment of mind. Both of those alternatives are impossible, for mind can only be produced by a previous moment of mind in its own continuum.By purifying our mindstream, we can make our future existence better than our present one.

What connects one life with the next? Is there a soul, atman, self, or real personality that goes from one life to another?

Our mind has gross and subtle levels. The sense consciousnesses that see, hear, smell, taste, and feel tactile sensations, and the gross mental consciousness, which is busy thinking this and that, actively function while we are alive. At the time of death, they cease to function and absorb into the subtle, and finally the extremely subtle, mental consciousness. This extremely subtle mind bears the imprints of our actions (karma). After death, the continuity of the subtle mind, which is neither static nor an independent entity, leaves one body, enters the intermediate state, and then takes rebirth in another body. After the subtle mind joins with another body at the moment of conception, the gross sense consciousnesses and the gross mental consciousness reappear, and the person again sees, hears, thinks, and so forth. This extremely subtle mind, which goes from one life to the next, is a constantly changing, dependent phenomenon. For this reason, it is not considered to be a soul, atman, self, or real personality. Thus the Buddha taught the doctrine of selflessness—that there is no solid, independent, findable thing that can be isolated as the person.

Do plants have minds? Are they sentient beings? Could a computer ever become a sentient being?

In general, according to Tibetan Buddhism, plants are not sentient beings. They are biologically alive, but that doesn't mean they are conscious. Plants may react to music or to people talking to them, just as iron filings react to a magnet placed near them, but that doesn't indicate that they have minds. However, in some rare cases, due to one's past actions, a person's mind may be attracted to a tree, for example, as its habitat.

When asked whether computers could ever have consciousness, His Holiness the Dalai Lama responded that if at some point computers had the ability to act as a physical support for consciousness and if a person had created the karma to be reborn inside one, then a computer could become a sentient being!

Is there one universal mind that we are all a part of?

According to Buddhism, no. Each of us has our own mindstream. However, when we purify our minds and become Buddhas, we will no longer have the feeling of being separate, isolated individuals. We will each be an individual Buddha, but we will have the same spiritual realizations. We won't feel cut off from each other.

Where did ignorance come from? Were we once enlightened and then became separated from that state?

No. Once someone is enlightened, there is no cause to again become confused and ignorant. If the cause for imperfection exists in the mind, the person is still ignorant. Thus from a Buddhist viewpoint, we weren't once enlightened and then fell from that state. Such an occurrence is impossible because there's no cause for it to happen.

Although all sentient beings have Buddha nature or Buddha potential, their minds have been clouded over by ignorance since beginningless time. Each moment of ignorance was produced from the preceding moment, without beginning. No external being created it. However, although ignorance has no beginning, it does have an end. It can be removed through the wisdom realizing emptiness, the lack of fantasized ways of existing. Once we perceive reality, our minds can no longer ignorantly misconceive things.

What is Buddha nature?

Buddha nature or Buddha potential is the potential that all sentient beings have to become fully enlightened. This is an inseparable part of our mind, and awareness of it gives us a firm foundation for self-confidence and hope. Our Buddha nature is compared to the open expansive sky that is always there. Clouds may temporarily obscure it, but since the clouds and the sky are not of the same nature, the clouds can be removed. Similarly, the deeper nature of our mind is pure, but it is temporarily obscured by circumstantial defilements of the disturbing attitudes, negative emotions, and subtle stains. When these are eliminated through practicing the path, we become fully enlightened Buddhas.

Why can't we remember our past lives?

At the moment, our minds are obscured by ignorance, making it difficult to remember the past. Also, many changes occur in our body and mind as we die and are reborn, making recollection difficult. However, the fact that we don't remember something doesn't mean that it does not exist. Sometimes we cannot even remember where we put our car keys! Nor can we remember what we ate for dinner a month ago!

Some people can remember their past lives. The Tibetans have a system of recognizing the reincarnations of highly realized masters. Quite often, as young children, these people will recognize their friends or possessions from a previous life. Some ordinary people have also had past life recall, sometimes in meditation or through hypnosis. For example, as a child, a woman in Britain remembered the village in which she lived in her previous life and would draw pictures of it. She also recalled her family there: she was the mother of eight children. When she was an adult, she went to that village and met her son from the previous life who was now in his seventies. He was able to validate many of her previous life memories because he remembered the same events from his childhood.

Is it important to know what our past lives were?

No. What's important is how we live our present life. Knowing what we were in past lives is useful only if it helps us to generate strong determination to avoid negative actions or to free ourselves from cyclic existence. To try to find out who we were in past lives only for curiosity's sake isn't useful. It could even lead us to become proud: "I was a king in my past life." "I was so famous and talented." "I was Einstein!" So what? Actually, we have all been and done everything in our infinite past lives in cyclic existence. The important thing is to purify our previous negative actions, avoid creating more, and put energy into accumulating positive potential and developing our good qualities.

There's a Tibetan saying: "If you want to know about your past life, look at your present body. If you want to know your future life, look at your present mind." We received our present rebirth as a result of our past actions. A human rebirth is a fortunate one, and we created the cause for it by living ethically in our previous lives. These good causes were probably created in a fortunate rebirth in the past, because creating such virtue is difficult in unfortunate rebirths. On the other hand, our future rebirths will be determined by what we think, say, and do now, and our mind motivates all these actions. Thus, we can get an idea of the kind of rebirths we will take by looking at our present attitudes and emotions and examining whether they are constructive or destructive. We don't need to go to a fortuneteller to ask what will become of us. We can simply consider the imprints we are leaving on our mindstream moment by moment by our thoughts, words, and deeds.

If everyone has had previous lives, how do you account for the population increase?

All the people alive now weren't necessarily human beings on planet Earth in their past lives. Their previous lives could have been as another life-form or in another universe. Earth is a tiny speck in the universe, and Buddhists believe that there is life in other places. Also, an animal, for example, could die and be reborn as a human.

Chapter Eight

KARMA: THE FUNCTIONING OF CAUSE AND EFFECT

What is karma? How does it work?

Karma means action, and refers to intentional physical, verbal, or mental actions. These actions leave imprints or seeds upon our mindstreams, and the imprints ripen into our experiences when the appropriate conditions come together. For example, with a kind heart we help someone. This action leaves an imprint on our mindstream, and when conditions are suitable, this imprint will ripen as our receiving help when we need it. If an action brings about pain and misery in the long term, it is called negative, destructive, or nonvirtuous. If it brings about happiness, it is called positive, constructive, or virtuous. Actions aren't inherently good or bad, but are only designated so according to the results they bring.

All results come from causes that have the ability to create them. If we plant apple seeds, an apple tree will grow, not chili. If chili seeds are planted, chili will grow, not apples. In the same way if we act constructively, happiness will ensue; if we act destructively, problems will result. Whatever happiness and fortune we experience in our lives comes from our own positive actions, while our problems result from our own destructive actions.

The seeds of our actions continue with us from one lifetime to the next and do not get lost. However, if we don't create the cause or karma for something, then we won't experience that result: if a farmer doesn't plant seeds, nothing will grow.

Is the law of actions and their effects a system of punishment and reward? Did the Buddha create or invent it?

Definitely not. According to Buddhism, there is no one in charge of the universe who distributes rewards and punishments. We create the causes by our actions, and we experience their results. We are responsible for our own experience. The Buddha didn't create the system of actions and their effects, in the same way that Newton didn't invent gravity. Newton simply described what exists. Likewise, the Buddha described what he saw with his omniscient mind to be the natural process of cause and effect occurring within the mindstream of each being. By doing this, he showed us how best to work within the functioning of cause and effect in order to experience happiness and avoid pain.

The misconception that happiness and pain are rewards and punishments may come from incorrect translations of Buddhist scriptures into English. I have seen some translations that use terminology from other religions. This is very misleading because terms such as heaven, hell, sin, punishment, and judgment do not correspond to Buddhist concepts. Appropriate English words that convey the meaning of the Buddha's teachings must be used.

Does the law of actions and their effects apply only to people who believe in it?

No. Cause and effect functions whether we believe in it or not. Positive actions produce happiness and destructive ones result in pain whether we believe they will or not. If a fruit drops from a tree, it falls down even if we believe it will go up. It would be wonderful if all we needed to do to avoid the results of our actions was to believe they wouldn't come! Then, for example, we could eat all we want and never get fat! People who don't believe in past lives and cause and effect still experience happiness as a result of their actions in past lives. But by denying the existence of cause and effect, and consequently not attempting to practice constructive actions and avoid destructive ones, they may create few positive potentials and recklessly create many negative ones. On the other hand, people who know about cause and effect will try to be mindful of what they think, say, and do to avoid hurting others and to avoid leaving harmful imprints on their own mindstreams.

What does karma affect?

Karma can affect our future rebirths, that is, the kind of life-form we will adopt. It also influences what we experience during our lives: how others treat us, our wealth, social status, and so forth. In addition, karma affects our personality and character: our talents, dominant personality traits, and habits. What kind of environment we're born into is also influenced by karma.

Why do some people who act destructively appear to be successful and happy? Why do some people who don't believe in the functioning of cause and effect have good lives?

When we see dishonest people who are wealthy, or cruel people who are powerful, or kind people who die young, we may doubt the law of actions and their effects. This is because we are looking only at the short period of this one life. Many of the results we experience in this life are the results of actions done in previous lives, and many of the actions we do in this life will ripen only in future lives. The wealth of dishonest people is the result of their generosity in preceding lives. Their current dishonesty leaves the karmic seed for them to be cheated and to experience poverty in future lives. Likewise, the respect and authority given to cruel people is due to positive actions they did in the past. In the present, they are misusing their power, thus creating the cause for future pain. Kind people who die young are experiencing the result of negative actions done in past lives. However, their present kindness is planting seeds or imprints on their mindstreams for them to experience happiness in the future.

The Buddhist scriptures outline general guidelines about the results of various actions. However, only a Buddha's omniscient mind can completely understand the specific details of the ripening of karma. For example, the scriptures tell us that killing causes a short life and generosity results in wealth. But we ordinary beings aren't capable of knowing for certain who our friend Susan was in a past life, to whom she was generous, and what she gave that resulted in her being rich in this life.

There is flexibility in the functioning of actions and their results. While we know that insulting others, for example, brings an unfortunate rebirth, just exactly what body we're born into can vary. If the action was very heavy—for example, with strong anger we repeatedly abused many people and afterward felt gratified that we had hurt their feelings—the result will be more unpleasant than if we casually teased someone once and later regretted our insensitivity. The conditions present at the time that karmic seed ripens will also influence what specific result it brings.

Do we create karma together as a group?

Yes. Karma may be either collective and individual. Collective karma are the actions we do together as a group. For example, soldiers use weapons, a group of religious practitioners pray or meditate. The results of these actions are experienced together as a group, often in future lives. Yet each member of a group thinks, speaks, and acts slightly differently, thus creating individual karma, the results of which each person will experience him or herself.

Do we necessarily experience the results of all of our actions?

When seeds, even small ones, are planted in the ground, they will eventually sprout—that is, unless they do not receive the necessary conditions for growth such as water, sunshine, and fertilizer, or they are burnt or pulled out of the ground. The ultimate way to uproot karmic imprints or seeds is by meditating on the emptiness of inherent existence. At our level, this may be rather difficult, but we can still stop the harmful seeds from ripening by purifying them. This is similar to preventing the seed from receiving water, sunshine, and fertilizer.

How can we purify negative imprints?

Purification by means of the four opponent powers is very important. It not only prevents future suffering, but also relieves guilt. By cleansing our minds, we will be more peaceful and will be able to concentrate and to understand the Dharma better. The four opponent powers used to purify negative imprints or seeds are:

1) Regret
2) Determination not to do the action again
3) Taking refuge and generating an altruistic attitude toward others
4) An actual remedial practice

First, we acknowledge and regret that we have acted destructively. This is different from self-recrimination and guilt, which are useless and keep us bound up in anxiety. With sincere regret, on the other hand, we simply acknowledge our mistake and regret having made it.

Secondly, we make a determination not to do the action again. If the action is habitual and frequent—for example, criticizing others—it would be hypocritical to say we will never do it again for the rest of our lives. It's better to resolve that we will try not to repeat the action again, but will be especially mindful and make a concerted effort during a realistic, set period of time, such as a few days. In this way, we will also develop confidence that we can do what we promise to.

The third opponent power is to take refuge and generate altruism. Our destructive actions are generally in relation to either holy entities such as the Buddhas, Dharma, and Sangha, or other sentient beings. To reestablish a good relationship with the holy objects, we seek their guidance by taking refuge in them. To restore our good relationships with other sentient beings, we generate an altruistic attitude towards them by aspiring to become a Buddha so we can best benefit them.

The fourth opponent power is remedial action. This may be any positive action: listening to teachings, reading a Dharma book, bowing to the Three Jewels, making offerings, reciting the names of the Buddhas, chanting mantras, making statues or paintings of the Buddhas, printing texts, meditating, and so on. We may also offer service in the community, aiding those in difficulty by doing volunteer work in schools, hospitals, or environmental organizations. Or, we may offer service to a Dharma center or temple. The most powerful remedial action is to meditate on emptiness because nonconceptual wisdom uproots the negative imprints so that they can never bear fruit.

The four opponent powers must be done repeatedly. We have acted harmfully many times, so we cannot expect to counteract these seeds at once. The stronger the four opponents powers are—the stronger our regret, the firmer our determination not to do the action again, and so on—the more powerful the purification will be. It's especially effective to purify ourselves using the four opponent powers every evening before going to sleep to counteract any destructive actions we have done during the day.

If people suffer because of their own negative actions, does that mean that we cannot or should not do anything to help them?

Not at all! We know what it's like to feel miserable, and that is exactly how others feel when they are experiencing the results of their own destructive actions. Out of empathy and compassion, we should definitely help! Their present predicament was brought about by their own actions, but that doesn't mean that we should stand by and say, "Oh that's too bad. You poor thing. You shouldn't have done such destructive actions."

Karma isn't inflexible or cast in concrete. It doesn't mean fate or predetermination. People may have created the cause to experience difficulties, but they also may have created the cause to receive help from us! Even more than that, we all know how we would feel if we were in such a situation. We are all alike in wanting happiness and trying to avoid pain. It doesn't matter whose pain or problem it is, we must try to relieve it. For example, to think, "The poor are poor because of their own miserliness in past lives. I would be interfering with their karma if I tried to help." is a cruel misconception. We should not rationalize our own laziness, apathy, or smugness by misinterpreting cause and effect. Compassion and universal responsibility are important for our own spiritual development and for world peace. They are the cornerstones of all Buddhist practice.

Does karma influence whom we will meet and the relationships we'll have with them?

Yes, but this doesn't mean those relationships are predetermined. We may have certain karmic predispositions to feel close to or to have friction with certain people. Nevertheless, these relationships may not continue along those same lines. If we are kind to those who speak ill of us and try to communicate effectively with them, the relationships will change. We'll also create positive karma, which will bring happiness in the future.

We are not karmically bound to others. Nor are there "soul mates," special people who are the one and only one for us. Since we've had infinite past lives, we've had contact with every being sometime before. Also, our relationship with any particular person constantly changes.

Nonetheless, past karmic connections can influence our present relationships. For example, if someone has been our spiritual mentor in a past life, we may be drawn to that person this lifetime, and his or her teaching the Dharma may have a very strong effect on our minds.

Can understanding karma help us to understand the events in our lives better?

Yes, it can. The happiness we experience comes from our previously created positive actions. Understanding this encourages us to act constructively and not sit back passively when opportunities to be kind appear.

When we experience some difficulties in life, we should reflect on the type of action we must have done that created the cause for this result. This will encourage us to be more aware of what we think, say, and do. Studying the Buddha's teachings enables us to learn more about specific actions and their results. Then we can change our behavior and plant more seeds in our mindstreams to experience desirable results. A text called *The Wheel of Sharp Weapons* is particularly good in explaining the effects produced by certain actions and the way to change our attitudes and actions to create the cause of happiness.

Can people be reborn as animals and animals as people? How is that karmically possible?

Yes. Based on our actions, our minds are attracted toward certain types of rebirth when we die. It may seem difficult to imagine that a human being could be reborn as an animal, but if we consider the fact that some people act worse than animals, it doesn't seem so far-fetched. For example, animals kill only when they are threatened or hungry, while some human beings kill for sport, fame, or power. If someone's mind habitually goes in a certain direction, it makes sense that his or her body could correspond to that mental state in a future life.

Similarly, animals can be reborn as humans. Although it's difficult for most animals to do many positive actions—it's hard to teach a dog to meditate or to offer community service—it is possible. For this reason, Tibetans take their animals when they circumambulate holy monuments in order to put good imprints on the animals' minds. Many people enjoy saying their prayers or mantras out loud so their pets can hear them and be exposed to such soothing sounds, even though the animals do not understand the meaning.

Ordinary people have both positive and negative karmic imprints on their minds. What rebirth we take is not a sum total of all of our past karma. Rather, certain seeds ripen while others remain dormant. Thus, if someone is angry at the time he dies, some of the negative imprints could ripen and he could be reborn as a dog. However, the positive imprints still remain on his mindstream and when causes and conditions come together, they could ripen, causing him to again be reborn as a human.

Chapter Nine

DYING, DEATH, AND THE INTERMEDIATE STATE

How can we best help someone who is dying or dead?

When people are terminally ill, we should help them arrange their worldly affairs while their bodies and minds are still strong. In this way, they can put to rest their worries and concerns about money and family. It's helpful if they can give away their belongings because they create much good karma through generosity and this will help them in future lives. Generosity also frees them from attachment, which is very harmful at the time of death. We should encourage them to resolve any grudges or remorse they may have, either by discussing their feelings with the people concerned or by doing purification practices. Apologizing, forgiving, and telling those they love that they love them can help to free their minds from anger and guilt and enable them to die peacefully.

If we cannot help people prepare for death in this way, then as death approaches, we should assure them that their worldly affairs will be taken care of after they pass away. They need not be concerned about who will pay the bills or take care of the children. They should concentrate on leaving this life peacefully, without fears or worries. Don't bother people by asking, "Who will get your jewelry?" "Do you have any hidden money?" or "How will I live without you?" Our motivation is to help dying people, not to give them more problems!

When people are dying, create an environment that is calm and free from people and things that could evoke their attachment or anger. Dying peacefully is difficult if the entire family is in the room crying, grasping the person's hand, and pleading, "Please don't die. We love you. How can you leave us?" We may think we are expressing our love and concern by acting this way, but actually, our selfish mind is wailing because we're losing someone we care about. We should try to care more about the dying person's needs than our own and make the environment calm and pleasant.

During a person's final hours before death, it is recommended to discontinue all invasive treatment—monitors, IVs and so on. This allows the person to turn his or her thoughts inward and prepare to die without being distracted by external commotion. It also permits the physical energies to dissolve in a more natural way.

Dying with anger, attachment, jealousy, or pride as their last thought is harmful. Thus, we should try to create a quiet and calm environment and encourage them to generate positive thoughts. If they are Buddhist, we can talk about the Buddha, Dharma, and Sangha and remind them of their spiritual masters. We should show them pictures of the Buddha or chant prayers and mantras in the room. Before death actually occurs, encourage them to purify their destructive actions. Tell them to pray for a good rebirth, to meet pure teachings and teachers, and to make their death, intermediate state and rebirth beneficial for others.

If people are of other faiths, do not push your faith on them at the time of death. That causes confusion in their minds. Rather, speak according to their faith and encourage them to generate positive states of mind.

Are people reborn immediately after death or is there an intermediate state before the next rebirth?

The heart and breath may stop and people may be brain-dead, but their subtlest consciousness may still remain connected to the body for up to three days. Highly realized masters may even meditate for weeks after their vital signs have ceased, before their subtlest consciousness leaves their body. For that reason, it's recommended to leave the body undisturbed for several days or at least for a few hours if possible. Then, touch the crown of the person's head, because the consciousness leaving from that point is auspicious for the next life.

After an ordinary person's mind leaves the gross physical body, it enters an intermediate stage (*bardo* in Tibetan) before it assumes another gross body. Depending on conditions, a person may remain in the intermediate stage for only a few moments, or for as long as forty-nine days. In certain cases, the person is reborn immediately, without staying in the intermediate state. Although I've asked several teachers, I haven't discovered why the *bardo* must cease after forty-nine days, rather than another number of days.

Beings in the intermediate state have subtle bodies that are not made of atoms but are similar to the being they will become. For a short time they may try to communicate with their friends or relatives from their previous life, but intermediate state beings are not able to communicate with human beings. After forty-nine days they have definitely taken new bodies and are absorbed in the experiences of their new lives.

Can someone be reborn as a spirit? How do we account for channeling or for people who talk to a dead relative through a medium?

Some people have created the causes to be reborn as spirits. Spirits belong to a realm of life-forms called hungry ghosts, which is considered an unfortunate rebirth. Spirits and sometimes gods can channel through mediums, but all these beings are still bound to cyclic existence by their ignorance, attachment, and anger. Some may have clairvoyant powers, some may not; some may tell the truth, some may not. Spiritual channeling is not always reliable. There's no need to contact dead friends and relatives. It's more worthwhile to communicate well with them and be kind to them now, while they're alive.

Does chanting for the dead help? What else can be done for them?

After death, chanting the sutras and doing other Buddhist practices can be helpful by stimulating the deceased's own positive potential to ripen. Although they have already left their physical body and can't hear the chanting with their ears, our creating positive potential and dedicating it to their welfare can help. Traditionally, such virtuous practices are done each week for seven weeks after a death. Until they find another gross body to take rebirth in, they remain in the intermediate stage. The positive potential we create and dedicate for them can help them find a good rebirth. However, don't think, "I'll ask some monks and nuns to do the chanting while I go about my business." We have a karmic relationship with the deceased, so the prayers and virtuous activities that we dedicate for their benefit are important too.

It's helpful to offer the deceased's possessions to others as a way of practicing generosity and accumulating positive potential. Offering to holy objects (Buddha, Dharma, Sangha) and to the poor and sick is especially beneficial. We can then dedicate the positive potential from this for the benefit of all sentient beings and especially for the deceased.

Some Asians leave out food for the deceased and burn paper money and houses for the deceased. Is this necessary or beneficial?

It's said that intermediate state beings survive by "eating" smells, so leaving out food may be helpful during the forty-nine days after death. After that the deceased have been reborn in a happy or unfortunate rebirth according to their previous actions. After they have been born, the food set out never reaches them. Most likely there is food available wherever they have been reborn. However, we can offer food to beings born as hungry ghosts—be they our former relatives and friends or not—by reciting certain mantras over extra food. These mantras help to eliminate the hungry ghosts' karmic obscurations to finding food.

Burning paper cars, clothes, or money doesn't give the deceased these things in their future rebirth. The tradition of doing so is an old Chinese custom, not a practice taught by the Buddha. If we want to help our relatives and friends to have wealth in their future lives, we should encourage them to make offerings and be generous while they are alive. The Buddha said generosity, not burning paper objects, is the cause of wealth.

Sometimes, we may advise our relatives, "Don't give away so much. Our family won't have as much money if you do." By encouraging them to be miserly, we cause them to plant seeds in their mindstreams to be poor in their future lives. Also, we plant the same kind of seeds in our own mindstreams. On the other hand, encouraging them to be generous and to avoid cheating others in business helps them to be wealthy in the future.

If we want our loved ones to have a good rebirth, the best help we can give is to encourage them while they are alive to avoid the ten destructive actions and to practice the ten constructive ones, which are their opposites. The ten destructive actions are killing, stealing, unwise sexual behavior, lying, slander, harsh speech, gossip, coveting others' possessions, maliciousness, and wrong views. If we encourage them to lie to protect us or to cheat someone so we can have more money, we're helping them to create the cause for unfortunate rebirths. Should we spend hours gossiping with them, drinking, and criticizing others, we're defeating our own purpose. Since we sincerely want our relatives and friends to be happy after death, we should help them abandon these destructive actions and practice constructive ones. We can encourage (but not force) them to take ethical precepts. That is really acting to benefit their future lives.

What is the Buddhist view on suicide?

Suicide is considered a great tragedy. Human life is precious and it's a tragedy when people become so overwhelmed by their disturbing attitudes that they see death as the only way to stop their suffering. In fact, suicide doesn't really solve their problems because they will be reborn. Also, people who kill themselves are generally experiencing great anger, jealousy, or other disturbing attitudes at the time of death, and this could adversely affect their future rebirth.

Buddhists believe that all sentient beings have the Buddha potential, or Buddha nature, the potential to become fully enlightened. The disturbing attitudes are like clouds obscuring the pure nature of our minds, but they aren't part of us. They are fleeting, and through Dharma practice, we can remove them entirely. If people could get even an inkling of this, they wouldn't take their own misery so seriously and would be confident in their own inner goodness. This new perspective may help them decide to continue living because they recognize a reliable way to stop their problems.

What is the Buddhist view on euthanasia?

From the Buddhist viewpoint, preserving life is generally recommended. However, each situation is different and must be looked at individually. In many cases, there are no easy answers. If we know that a person who is comatose or who is in great pain will be reborn in a happier situation, then, motivated by compassion, we could consider mercy killing. However, as most of us lack such clairvoyance, it's extremely difficult to know whether we would be helping or harming another by mercy killing. The seed of a previous negative action could possibly ripen, causing that person to be reborn in a situation which is worse than the present one. Sometimes people come out of coma and live for many years.

If people understand the value of human life—how precious it is for practicing the path to enlightenment—they may be able to transform painful situations into the path. For example, people may be bedridden, but if their minds are alert, they can practice the Dharma, increase their good qualities, purify their negative actions, and practice the path to enlightenment. In fact, they may have more time to do this than people who are busy running here and there! Some Buddhist practices are especially designed for transforming adverse conditions into the path, and we teach them to people who are very ill. Also, I have spoken to people who have been in comas, and several of them said that they were aware of their environment. Thus, reading prayers or reciting mantras near comatose people could help them. Even if their minds are obscured, hearing the Dharma leaves beneficial imprints on their minds.

When people make "living wills" stating their preferences for medical treatment if they are severely injured or ill, it reduces their family's anxiety should such unfortunate events occur. Not putting someone on life support when there is no hope for his or her recovery is not an act of killing. This is simply letting nature take its course, and it may allow the person to die more peacefully than if invasive or forceful measures were employed. However, once someone is on a life-support system, the issue becomes more complicated. Each situation needs to be considered separately because many factors are involved: the dying person's own wishes, the severity of their condition, the person's level of conscious awareness, his or her spiritual preparedness for death and emotional state, and the emotional and financial toll on the family. There is no one answer suitable for all cases. We must act with as much compassion and wisdom as possible when faced with such difficult decisions.

Because funding for medical research and health care is limited, our society could allocate most of those funds to improve prenatal care and education, thus improving the quality of life. In this way, people would not be faced with so many ethical and emotional dilemmas near the time of death.

Chapter Ten

THE BUDDHIST TRADITIONS

What are the Buddhist scriptures called?

The scriptures spoken by the Buddha fall into two general categories: the sutras and the tantras. The sutras deal with the Higher Trainings of Ethical Discipline, Meditative Stabilization, and Wisdom as well as the development of altruism and the general practices undertaken with that motivation. The tantras describe practices unique to Vajrayana. The Buddha spoke both the sutras and tantras during his lifetime, but to different audiences. His direct disciples memorized them and later generations recorded them in writing.

Why are there many Buddhist traditions?

The Buddha gave a wide variety of teachings because sentient beings (beings with mind who are not yet Buddhas) have different dispositions, inclinations, and interests. The Buddha never expected everyone to fit into the same mold. Thus, with skill and compassion in guiding others, he offered several philosophical systems and ways of practicing so that each of us could find something that suits our inclinations and personality. The essence of all his teachings is the same: the determination to be free from cyclic existence; love, compassion and altruism toward others; and the wisdom realizing reality.

Not everyone likes the same kind of food. At a huge buffet dinner, we can choose the dishes we like. Although we may have a taste for sweets, that doesn't mean that the salty dishes aren't good and should be thrown away! Similarly, we may prefer a certain approach to the teachings: Theravada, Pure Land, Zen, Vajrayana, and so on. We are free to choose the approach that suits us best and with which we feel the most comfortable. However, maintaining an open mind and respect for other traditions is important. As our minds develop, we may come to understand elements in other traditions that we failed to comprehend previously. In short, we should practice whatever we find useful to help us live a better life, and we can leave aside without criticizing whatever we do not yet understand.

Although we may find one particular tradition best suited for our personality, it's not wise to identify with it too strongly: "*I* am a Mahayanaist, *you* are a Theravadin," or "*I* am a Buddhist, *you* are a Christian." We are all human beings who seek happiness and want to realize the truth, and we each must find a method that suits our disposition.

However, while keeping an open mind to different approaches, we should avoid mixing everything together at random, making our practice like chop suey. It's best not to do meditation techniques from different traditions together in one meditation session, but in each session to stick to the techniques taught in one tradition. If we take a little of this technique and a little from that and mix them together without understanding either one very well, we may end up confused. Nevertheless, a teaching emphasized in one tradition may enrich our understanding and practice of another.

In addition, it is advisable to do the same meditation daily. If we do breathing meditation one day, chanting the Buddha's name the next, and analytical meditation the third, we won't make progress in any of them for we lack continuity in practice. However, we can do all three each day, thus maintaining continuity in our practice.

What are the various Buddhist traditions?

Generally, there are two divisions: Theravada and Mahayana. The Theravada lineage (Tradition of the Elders), which relies on sutras recorded in the Pali language, spread from India to Sri Lanka, Thailand, Burma, and other southeast Asian countries. It emphasizes meditation on the breath to develop concentration and meditation on mindfulness of the body, feelings, mind, and phenomena in order to develop wisdom. In Pali, these two types of meditation are called shamatha and vipassana.

The Mahayana (Great Vehicle) tradition, based on the scriptures recorded in Sanskrit, spread to China, Tibet, Japan, Korea, and Vietnam. Although love and compassion are essential and important factors in Theravada Buddhism, they are emphasized to an even greater extent in Mahayana Buddhism. Within Mahayana, there are several branches. Pure Land emphasizes chanting the name of Amitabha Buddha in order to be reborn in his pure land, a place where all conditions are conducive to Dharma practice. Zen (Ch'an) emphasizes meditation to eliminate the noisy, conceptual mind. Vajrayana (Diamond Vehicle) employs meditation on a deity in order to transform our contaminated body and mind into those of a Buddha. These are just a few examples of the many schools in Mahayana.

The fact that there are a variety of practices within the Buddhist doctrine attests to the Buddha's skill in guiding people according to their dispositions and needs. It is extremely important not to be partial and sectarian, but to have respect for all the traditions and their practitioners. Since the teaching of all these traditions originate from the Buddha, if we disparage one tradition, we are disparaging the Buddha and his teachings.

Why do some monks and nuns wear saffron robes while others dress in maroon, gray, or black?

As the Buddha's teachings spread from one country to another, they adapted to the culture and mentality of the people in each place without changing the essential meaning. The style of the sangha's robes is an external form, not the actual internal meaning of the teaching, thus it may change. In Sri Lanka, Thailand, Burma, Cambodia, and Laos for example, the robes are various shades of saffron and do not have sleeves. The climate and culture in those countries enabled them to retain the color and design of the robes from the Buddha's time. People who have taken the eight precepts and aren't technically monks or nuns wear white robes.

Saffron dye wasn't available in Tibet, so a deeper color, maroon, was used. In China it was considered impolite to expose the skin, so the long-sleeved costume of the T'ang Dynasty was adopted. Also, the Chinese considered saffron too bright for those on a religious path and only the emperor was permitted to wear golden-colored clothes. Thus, in China the color of the robes was changed to gray or black. However, the spirit of the original robes was kept in the form of the five, seven, and nine-piece brown, yellow and red outer robes that the monks and nuns wear while praying.

Why do the rituals differ from one tradition to the next?

Chanting styles vary in the various Buddhist countries in correspondence to the culture and language of the place. The musical instruments and the way of bowing differ as well. For example, the Chinese stand up while chanting, while the Tibetans sit down. These variations are due to cultural adaptations.

Similarly, the internal design of the temples may vary according to the place. Generally, temples have a statue of Shakyamuni Buddha in the center, and according to the tradition, other Buddhas, bodhisattvas, arhats, and Dharma protectors may also be depicted. The Tibetan environment was very stark, so they liked their temples to be very colorful and elaborately decorated inside. On the other hand, the Japanese landscape is lush, so they preferred the interiors of the temples to be simpler.

The external forms and ways of doing things are not the Dharma. They are tools to help us practice the Dharma better according to the culture and place in which we live. The real Dharma can't be seen with our eyes or heard with our ears. It is to be experienced by our minds and hearts. We must direct our attention to the real Dharma, not to the superficial appearances that may vary from place to place.

Chapter Eleven

VAJRAYANA

What is Vajrayana? What are the special qualities of Vajrayana practice?

Based upon the Theravada and general Mahayana practices, Vajrayana, also called Tantrayana, is a subdivision of the Mahayana. Vajrayana is widespread in Tibet and is practiced by the Japanese Shingon tradition as well.

One technique used in Vajrayana is visualizing oneself as a deity and the environment as the mandala or the environment of the deity. Using imagination in this way, Vajrayana practitioners transform their ordinary, poor self-image into that of a fully enlightened Buddha, and thus try to cultivate the noble qualities of the Buddhas in their own mindstreams. In other words, rather than getting locked into ordinary feelings of low self-esteem and lack of confidence, they imagine what it would feel like to be impartially compassionate toward all beings and to perceive the empty nature of all phenomena. Doing this functions psychologically to give them the energy and ability to progress along the path and actually develop those qualities.

Vajrayana contains techniques for transforming death, the intermediate state and rebirth into the body and mind of a Buddha. It also has special meditative techniques to develop calm abiding (*samatha*) as well as to make manifest an extremely subtle mind, which is used to realize emptiness. This extremely subtle wisdom mind can quickly and powerfully cleanse defilements from the mindstream. For this reason Vajrayana can bring enlightenment in this very lifetime if one is a qualified and well-trained student who practices under the guidance of a fully qualified tantric master.

Buddhist Tantra is not the same as Hindu Tantra, nor is it the practice of magic. Some people have written books about Vajrayana with incorrect information and interpretations. Therefore, if we wish to learn about this practice, we should either read books by knowledgeable authors or seek instruction from qualified masters.

What is an empowerment? Why are some teachings "secret"?

The purpose of empowerment (initiation) is to ripen one's mindstream for the tantric practice by making a connection with a deity who is a manifestation of the omniscient minds. This depends on having a virtuous motivation, taking the vows and commitments the empowerment entails, and meditating during the empowerment ceremony. Thus one does not receive empowerment merely by being present in the room where an empowerment is taking place. People may be present when an empowerment is offered, but if they do not take the vows and commitments at the appropriate times in the ceremony or meditate and visualize as the master instructs, they have not received the empowerment. Empowerment is not about having a vase placed on one's head, drinking blessed water, or tying a consecrated string around one's arm.

After empowerment, sincere practitioners seek instructions on how to do the practice. These instructions are not given before the empowerment because the students' minds are not yet prepared to practice them. For this reason they are "secret." It's not that the Buddha was miserly and didn't want to share the teachings, nor is tantric practice a membership to an exclusive club that jealously guards its secrets. Rather, tantric instruction is given only to people who have received empowerment to ensure that those engaging in the practice have been properly prepared. Otherwise, someone might misunderstand the symbolism employed in the tantra or engage in advanced and complex practices without proper preparation and instruction.

At what point does someone take a tantric empowerment?

Before entering the Vajrayana, one must be well trained in the determination to be free from cyclic existence, the altruistic intention, and the wisdom realizing the emptiness of inherent existence. One then takes an empowerment (initiation) from a qualified tantric master and follows the vows and commitments taken at the time of empowerment. On this basis, one receives instructions and practices the Vajrayana meditations. Initiations are not ends in themselves. They are a gateway into further practice. Thus sincere students take empowerments because they want to practice the teachings afterward.

Why are empowerments given so openly to newcomers if people need a firm foundation in general Buddhist practices to practice Tantra effectively?

Many lamas (Tibetan spiritual masters) believe that although people may not be fully prepared to do the Vajrayana practice, positive imprints are placed on their mindstreams by taking empowerments and thus making a karmic connection to the practice.

However, since taking tantric empowerments often involves taking vows and commitments and promising to do a certain meditation practice daily, it's wise for people to consider carefully before rushing into these practices. When Dharma centers announce an empowerment, they should also tell people which vows and commitments are involved and which practices must be done afterward. Also, people should examine the qualities of a spiritual master to make sure that he or she is qualified and that they want to form a teacher-student relationship with that person. Going slowly and developing one's Dharma practice gradually is best, rather than jumping into high practices thinking "this is the one and only opportunity." Also, one should avoid running here and there, taking every empowerment that is offered. It's better to take fewer empowerments but to practice them well, than to collect empowerments but practice very little.

Are there different types of empowerments?

Yes. In Tibetan, they fall into two main categories, *jenang* and *wong*. A *jenang* is like a blessing or permission to do the practice, while a *wong* entails actually imagining ourselves entering into the mandala of a deity. In English, both these terms are often translated as "initiation" or "empowerment," which is confusing. If you are unsure, ask the spiritual master giving it which it is.

In addition, the practice of each Buddha figure or deity has its own empowerment. Receiving empowerment into one practice does not enable us to do the practice of another deity. We must receive that deity's specific empowerment.

Why is the Kalachakra empowerment given publicly to a large number of people, many of whom may not even be Buddhists?

This empowerment is unique because the Kalachakra practice speaks about the welfare of the entire society, and it was first given centuries ago in order to unify and bring peace in a certain society. Thus, when His Holiness the Dalai Lama gives this empowerment, he offers non-Buddhists and Buddhists who are not yet ready to take an empowerment the option of attending the ceremony as a neutral observer, without taking the empowerment. This is done only in the case of this empowerment. At other times, we are not permitted to be a tourist in an empowerment, simply watching the proceedings.

What does the imagery in tantric art mean?

Vajrayana deals with transformation, and therefore symbolism is widely used. All the tantric deities are manifestations of fully enlightened, compassionate Buddhas, yet the appearance of some of these deities is ferocious or desirous. The sexual imagery isn't to be taken literally, according to worldly appearances. In Vajrayana, the depiction of deities in sexual union represents the union of method and wisdom, the two aspects of the path needed to attain enlightenment. Ferocious looking deities are not monsters who threaten us. Their wrath is directed toward ignorance and selfishness, which are our real enemies. This imagery, when properly understood, shows how desire and anger can be transformed and thereby subdued. It has deep meaning, far beyond ordinary lust and anger. One should avoid misinterpreting it.

What are mandalas?

There are many types of mandalas. In tantric practice, they are the mansions and environments of the various Buddhist deities. These mandalas, which are actually three dimensional, are often drawn like blueprints on a two-dimensional surface with sand or paint. Once we have received the appropriate empowerment, we may visualize the three-dimensional mandala of a deity as part of a meditation. Doing this practice entails receiving instructions from our spiritual master.

"Mandala" can also refer to the world and environment we live in. Thus, when we offer the mandala when requesting teachings, we visualize our universe and everything beautiful in it and offer this to our spiritual masters while requesting them to guide, instruct, and inspire us.

Who are dakas and dakinis?

They are tantric practitioners who aid others on the path. We generally visualize them in transcendental forms, but in some cases, they may appear as ordinary people.

Who are the Dharma protectors?

Dharma protectors are found in most Buddhist traditions, not just the Vajrayana. These are beings who have promised to help safeguard the existence of the Dharma in our world and to protect the people who practice it. They are generally fierce in appearance, but their wrath is directed toward the ignorance producing the misunderstandings, disharmony, and degeneration that destroy the Dharma. Some Dharma protectors are trans-worldly, that is, they are manifestations of Buddhas or they are arya bodhisattvas who have direct perception of emptiness. Others are beings within cyclic existence who have promised the Buddhas that they would protect the Dharma. While the trans-worldly Dharma protectors have directly realized emptiness, the worldly ones have not. Thus the latter are not considered part of the Three Jewels of refuge.

What are pujas?

"Puja" is a Sanskrit word meaning offering. Thus pujas are offering ceremonies that generally involve imagining a manifestation of the Buddha and making various offerings. Offerings are not made to win the deity's favor, as enlightened beings are already compassionate towards all impartially. Rather, they enable us to develop a mind that

delights in giving and to create positive potential—good karma—
from offering to enlightened beings. "Tsog" is a Tibetan word meaning "assembly" and is a specific type of offering made to the root and
lineage gurus, meditational deities, Three Jewels, dakas and dakinis,
and Dharma protectors.

**Vajrayana seems to be full of colorful and elaborate rituals. Where
is the meditation?**

Public Vajrayana ceremonies may appear very ritualistic, but the rituals are not ends in themselves. They are guided meditations in which
practitioners try to generate the meanings of the prayers in their minds.
When these same practices are done privately, practitioners can shorten
the recitations and pause for longer periods to practice concentration
and insight meditation, or to meditate on loving-kindness.

Chapter Twelve

STEPS ALONG THE PATH

What is an arhat (arahat)? What is nirvana (nibbana)?

An arhat is someone who has eliminated ignorance, disturbing attitudes, and negative emotions (anger, attachment, jealousy, pride, etc.) from his or her mind forever. In addition, he or she has purified all karma that could cause rebirth in cyclic existence (samsara). An arhat abides in a state of peace, which is called nirvana or liberation and is beyond all unsatisfactory experiences and confusion.

What is bodhi, or enlightenment?

In addition to eliminating ignorance, disturbing attitudes, and contaminated actions (karma) from their minds, Buddhas have also eliminated the subtle stains of these defilements and have fully developed the altruistic intention that cherishes others more than self. Thus Buddhas have attained full enlightenment, the state in which all defilements have been purified and all good qualities developed.

What is a bodhisattva?

A bodhisattva is someone who spontaneously and continuously has the wish to attain enlightenment for the benefit of sentient beings. By practicing the path, such a person will attain the state of Buddhahood.

Different levels of bodhisattvas exist, according to their level of realization. Some are not yet free from cyclic existence, while others are. The latter can then voluntarily continue to take birth in the world by the power of their compassion to help others. Buddhas can do this as well.

Do bodhisattvas give up attaining enlightenment and stay in this world to help others?

Some scriptures say that bodhisattvas vow to stay in cyclic existence and not attain enlightenment until all beings have been liberated from cyclic existence. This means that bodhisattvas' compassion for sentient beings is so strong that if it were beneficial, they would happily sacrifice their own liberation for that of others. However, bodhisattvas are also practical and realize that to help others most effectively, they need to become Buddhas themselves because only Buddhas have the full compassion, wisdom, and skill needed to fully benefit others. Thus bodhisattvas seek to attain full enlightenment, but when they do, they don't remain in a solitary blissful state and forget about others. They manifest in forms to guide others skillfully.

What is an arya, a superior, or noble one?

This is a person who has direct realization of emptiness. Such a realization occurs before one becomes an arhat or Buddha. With an arya's wisdom realizing emptiness, one eliminates ignorance, disturbing attitudes, contaminated karma, and their stains, thereby attaining liberation and enlightenment.

Chapter Thirteen

WORKING WITH EMOTIONS

What role do emotions play in Buddhist practice? Does the Buddha have emotions?

Some emotions are realistic and constructive, others aren't. Thus, some are to be cultivated on the path and others abandoned. The Buddha taught various antidotes to counteract negative emotions such as anger, attachment, jealousy, and pride. He also taught techniques to cultivate positive emotions such as love and compassion. According to Buddhism, love is the wish for all others to have happiness and its causes, and compassion is the wish for them to be free of all unsatisfactory conditions and their causes. Such love and compassion are extended equally to all beings, and the Buddha taught a step-by-step method for developing them.

Are all desires bad? What about the desire to attain nirvana or enlightenment?

This confusion occurs because sometimes the English word "desire" is used to translate two different Buddhist concepts. In English, "desire" is of different types. The desire that is problematic exaggerates the good qualities of an object, person, place, or idea and clings to it. Such desire is a form of attachment. An example is being very emotionally dependent on someone and clinging to him or her. When we look with a more balanced attitude, we see that the other person isn't nearly as fantastic as our attachment led us to believe.

On the other hand, the desire that spurs us to prepare for future lives or to attain nirvana or enlightenment is completely different.

Here we realize that better states of being are possible and develop a realistic aspiration to achieve them. No misconceptions are involved, nor is there clinging to the desired result.

Wouldn't life be boring without attachment?

No. In fact it's attachment that makes us restless and prevents us from enjoying things. For example, suppose we're attached to chocolate cake. Even while we're eating it, we're not tasting it and enjoying it completely. We're usually either criticizing ourselves for eating something fattening, comparing the taste of this chocolate cake to other cakes we've eaten in the past, or planning how to get another piece. In any case, we're not really experiencing the chocolate cake in the present.

On the other hand, without attachment, we can think clearly about whether we want to eat the cake, and if we decide to, we can eat it peacefully, tasting and enjoying every bite without craving for more or being dissatisfied because it isn't as good as we expected.

As we diminish our attachment, life becomes more interesting because we're able to open up to what's happening in each moment. For example, rather than wishing we were with the people to whom we're attached, we'll appreciate being with whomever we're spending time with at present. Instead of being attached to our physical appearance and consequently feeling constant dissatisfaction with how we look, we'll simply do what's needed to keep our body healthy and clean and will be satisfied with how we look.

How can we pursue a career without attachment to reputation and wealth? How can we do business and also be ethical?

If we deeply contemplate the transient and unpredictable nature of wealth, reputation, and worldly success, the belief that they'll bring us lasting happiness will fade. Then we can start to change our motivation for working. We can look at our work as service to society and as an opportunity to learn more about ourselves by interacting with others. Our work will thus become an occasion to practice the teachings that we meditate on. In this way, patience and cherishing others will not be traits we cultivate only in meditation, but qualities we develop in daily life.

If we diminish our attachment, living ethically will be easier. As our priorities change, we will be fair in our business dealings and will not backbite to climb the corporate ladder. Although some people think being unethical is necessary to succeed in business, one successful business executive told me that the opposite is the case. When we deal fairly with clients, they trust us, continue to do business with us, and bring in new customers. When we treat our colleagues respectfully, they generally reciprocate, and we will avoid becoming entangled in office politics. Should others mistreat us, we can work on practicing tolerance and developing better communication skills. Our feeling of being successful human beings will not depend on money and fame. We'll feel better about ourselves and have less guilt because we live ethically. That will actually save money, because we will not need to go to a psychiatrist for our emotional problems or a lawyer for our legal ones!

How can we deal with fear?

Fear is closely related to attachment. The more attached we are to someone or something, the more we fear not having it or being separated from it. For example, if we're very attached to and emotionally dependent on a particular person, we fear the relationship will end. If we're attached to money and financial security, we are anxious about not having enough. If we're attached to our image, we fear looking stupid in front of others.

On one hand, it's normal to have such concerns because we've been raised to be attached to these things. On the other hand, clinging makes us fearful and anxious. The solution isn't to abandon our friends, money, and reputation but to let go of the attachment to them. Then we can enjoy them free from fear.

Meditating on impermanence and seeing the transient nature of things helps us to let go of attachment and to set our priorities wisely. Imagining getting all the things we are attached to and then asking ourselves, "Now am I forever happy?" enables us to stop obsessing about the things and people we are attached to. As we let go of the attachment, our fear of not having or of losing these objects of attachment will naturally dissipate.

Can one be attached to Buddhism? What should we do if someone attacks our beliefs and criticizes the Dharma?

Each situation must be regarded individually. In general, if we feel, "They are criticizing *my* beliefs. They think *I* am stupid for believing that," we are clinging to our beliefs because we think, "These beliefs are good because they are *mine*. If someone criticizes them, they are criticizing *me*." Such an attitude isn't very productive and we'll be more peaceful if we abandon it. We are not our beliefs. If others disagree with our beliefs, it does not mean we are stupid.

Being open to what others say is useful. Let's not be attached to the name and label of our religion. We are seeking truth and happiness, not promotion of a religion because it happens to be ours. In addition, questioning the teachings is reasonable. The Buddha himself said we should check his teachings and not just believe in them blindly.

On the other hand, we should not automatically agree with everything someone else says. We should not abandon our beliefs and adopt theirs indiscriminately. If someone asks a question we cannot answer, it doesn't mean the Buddha's teachings are wrong. It simply means we don't know the answer and need to learn and contemplate more. We can then take the question to knowledgeable Buddhists and think about their answers. When others question our beliefs, they are actually helping us deepen our understanding of the Buddha's teachings by showing us what we do not yet understand. This inspires us to study the Dharma and reflect on its meaning.

We needn't defend our beliefs to someone else. If people ask questions with sincere interest and are open-minded and interested in a real exchange of views, talking with them can be mutually enriching. However, if people really don't want a response and just want to antagonize or confuse us, then dialogue is impossible. There is no need to feel defensive in front of such people—we don't have to prove anything to them. Even if we were to give them logical answers, they would not listen because they are involved with their own preconceptions. Without being rude, we can be quite firm and end the conversation.

What can we do about stress?

Stress can be caused by a number of factors, some external and some internal. When we are stressed because there's not enough time and we feel pressured, it's helpful to think about our priorities and decide what things are most important in our lives. Then we can choose to do those things and put the others on the back burner. When we're stressed because we don't have the ability to do something that's expected of us, we need to accept our limitations. We aren't failures because we lack certain abilities. We need to communicate honestly with the people who hold such expectations of us. When we're stressed due to illness or sudden changes in our living situation, it's helpful to reflect on impermanence—that everything in our world will change. Then we can adapt to the change rather than fight it.

Our stress is often due to not accepting the reality of a situation. We want it to be different or we want ourselves or others to be different. However, what is happening at the moment is what exists. Instead of rejecting the situation, which causes us more anxiety, we can accept it and work with it. Accepting whatever is happening isn't being fatalistic; it's being realistic. Having accepted the reality of the situation for what it presently is, we can still try to improve it in the future while remaining realistic about what is possible.

Calming the mind through breathing meditation counteracts stress. So does meditating on patience and compassion. Purification meditation is helpful as well. For this reason, daily meditation is recommended to prevent and counteract stress.

Many people suffer from guilt and self-blame. What can be done about this?

Whether we made an error intentionally or not, guilt and self-hatred are inappropriate. We need to clearly examine what we are responsible for—what we have power over—and what we are not. Guilt often comes from considering ourselves responsible for something we have no power over. For example, if we find ourselves in a dangerous situation through our own carelessness, we are responsible for our being there. However, if someone physically or sexually abuses us, we are not responsible for this. It's the other's action, not our own. Abused children or rape-victims are not responsible for their own abuse or rape. There is no need to feel guilty or blame oneself for what happened.

If we deliberately cause another harm—for example by intentionally causing discord in our workplace—the pain that results is our doing. However, if we act with good intentions, yet another experiences pain from our actions, that is not our responsibility. For example, if, with a kind heart we try to give people feedback on their actions and they get upset, that is not our responsibility. But if we fail to take care in how we express ourselves, we are responsible for our miscommunication and should attempt to correct it.

When we act negatively due to our own confusion and disturbing attitudes, we should not feel guilty and blame ourselves. Instead, we should try to remedy the situation as best we can and also do purification practices to counteract the negative karmic imprint on our mindstream. From the Buddhist viewpoint, guilt is a disturbing attitude: it does not see the situation clearly and is a form of self-centeredness. Emotionally beating up on ourselves does not alter the past or develop our potential. It only immobilizes us and makes us spiral downward into self-preoccupation. On the other hand, if we have confidence in our ability to improve because we know we have the potential to become fully enlightened, we will regret our mistakes and act positively in order to remedy the harmful effects of our actions.

Can meditation solve our emotional problems?

That depends on us, our teacher, and our meditation practice. In some cases it can. In others, it's more effective if people seek help from a therapist and use meditation as an adjunct.

How are Buddhism and therapy similar? How are they different?

Both seek to understand the functioning of the human mind. Both offer techniques to foster happiness and well-being through generating more constructive mental states. Both transmit these techniques to others through experienced guides, and both are composed of various sub-schools with slightly different approaches and emphases.

However, the end goals of therapy and Buddhism differ. Therapy seeks to help people be happy in this life, whereas Buddhism is concerned with their happiness in future lives and their lasting happiness through attaining liberation. Therapy doesn't regard ignorance, anger, and attachment as the root causes of difficulties and therefore as attitudes to be abandoned completely. Therapists often encourage people to be angry at those who have harmed them and to find more effective ways to obtain the things they're attached to. Buddhism, on the other hand, seeks to uproot anger, attachment, and selfishness from the mind altogether.

There are some differences in the methods employed in therapy and in Buddhism. Many therapies involve recollecting past traumatic experiences and reprocessing them in the present. However, Buddhism encourages students to identify general behavior patterns and apply antidotes to them. Remembering specific childhood experiences and reliving them is not seen as important. Some therapies are concerned with the contents of the clients' dreams, whereas Buddhism generally is not. Meditators are encouraged to identify dreams as dreams and to use the illusory nature of dreams as an analogy to how things appear to exist from their own side, while in fact they do not.

The roles of spiritual masters and therapists differ as well. Therapy takes place individually or in a small group where people discuss their specific problems with the therapist. Spiritual teachers usually instruct larger groups and the students are responsible for practicing what they are taught on their own. Of course, if students need individual counseling or have questions about Dharma practice, spiritual mentors are happy to see them. Spiritual mentors are interested in how their students' meditation is progressing and in how well they are integrating the Dharma into their daily lives.

Transference may occur both in one's relationship with a therapist and with a spiritual mentor. Depending on the awareness and level of practice of the therapist or teacher, counter-transference may also occur.

Psychology and Buddhism can learn a lot from each other, and interest in this dialogue is increasing. More research and discussion in this area are needed.

What is the Buddhist position regarding antidepressants and other medications that are taken for mental unhappiness?

Each case must be examined separately, and the following are general guidelines. Depression is often caused by a combination of a chemical imbalance in the brain and psychological difficulties. When people are severely depressed, medications can enable them to feel well enough to begin to look at the psychological components of their depression. There is no stigma attached to taking antidepressants when they are needed to counteract a chemical imbalance in the brain or to help someone feel well enough to function in daily life. However, taking antidepressants in order to avoid looking at the psychological aspects of the depression is not helpful. Similarly, taking antidepressants for mild depression instead of examining and changing other factors contributing to the depression such as physical health, lack of exercise, poor diet, stressful factors in life, incorrect ways of interpreting events, and so on—is not recommended.

Chapter Fourteen

DHARMA IN DAILY LIFE

How can we live as Buddhists in modern society when its values and activities are so different from those we try to cultivate in our practice?

The more we think about the Buddha's teachings and become confident in their validity, the easier practice will become. For example, the more we examine our own experience and recognize the disadvantages of being attached to material possessions, the less power advertising will have over our minds. As we see the disadvantages of unethical actions, we won't get drawn into others' unwholesome schemes. Time and effort are necessary to integrate the Buddha's teachings in our minds, but as we do it, we will slowly progress.

Let's say we've decided to avoid taking intoxicants and our colleagues ask us to have a drink after work. We shouldn't launch into a harangue against drinking, but quietly order juice instead. We may initially feel embarrassed and fear ridicule, but this is due to our attachment to reputation. If we are clear about what we want and don't want to do, why be concerned with others' opinions? It could be that the others drink because they feel we expect them to, and they may be relieved when we don't! Even if they want to drink, a person who doesn't could be a good example to them.

The most important qualities necessary to live harmoniously with others are friendliness and genuine concern for others. The more we develop these internal qualities, the more they will automatically be reflected in our behavior and speech. Other people relate to and respect these qualities more than our sharing their views about such topics as intoxicants, the death penalty, and TV shows. If we are friendly, happy, and compassionate people, we will get along with others well.

How do we tell our family and friends who aren't Buddhist about our interest in the Dharma?

At the beginning of our practice, we tend not to be sure of ourselves or very confident in the Dharma, so we are very sensitive to others' comments about what we are doing. As we gradually relax into the practice, we'll find it easier to talk with our family, friends, and colleagues about Buddhism. Of course, we should not become preachers, using a lot of Buddhist jargon to impress others. Rather, we should answer people's questions simply, responding in a way that will make sense to them. There are many ways to talk about Buddhism without using Dharma words: after all, Buddhism is basically a common sense approach to life. When our friends talk to us about their problems, we can discuss the antidotes to anger, jealousy, or clinging attachment in a simple way without even using the word "Buddhism." Giving people more information than they want is not skillful. Therefore, we should listen carefully to someone's question and respond to it accurately without going on and on about unrelated or complicated topics that may interest us, but not the other person.

When talking with people of other religions, we can discuss the points that Buddhism has in common with their faith. Every religion values ethics, love, and compassion, so it's skillful to speak about these when first explaining Buddhism. Don't start off by talking about rebirth, karma, Buddha, Dharma, Sangha, and other unfamiliar words and concepts. Also, we can emphasize that according to Buddhism, the diversity of religions in the world is good because that gives people the opportunity to find a philosophy and practice that suits them. Everyone doesn't need to become a Buddhist. Speaking in this way makes people of other faiths relax, because they know we respect their beliefs and will not try to convert them.

Those who are married may want to invite their spouse and children to meet their teachers and Dharma friends or to visit their Dharma center if they're interested. Some people neglect their families because they've become excited about helping all sentient beings and becoming a Buddha. They practice patience with everyone but their spouse and children, and expect the rest of the family to do all the household chores while they meditate. This isn't very skillful! While Dharma practitioners want to lessen their clinging attachment to their families, they should not neglect them. Dharma involves generating genuine love and compassion for people we're in daily contact with, not just for sentient beings universes away whom we never see!

What can we do if our family and friends are not supportive or are even resentful of our interest in Buddhism?

First, accept that they feel that way and don't get angry about it. Being irritated at them will only increase the tension. On the other hand, we need not give up our beliefs or our practice due to family pressure. While flaunting our practice with a rebellious attitude is unwise, we need not hide it out of fear either. We can adapt to the external situation while keeping our practice alive and firm internally. For example, if our family cannot relate to a shrine with pictures of the Buddha, we can keep the pictures in our Dharma books and take them out when we meditate.

In many cases our actions will convince others of the value of our Dharma practice. When our colleagues notice that we're more patient and tolerant, they will be curious about what we've done to bring about this change. If we help to clean the house and take out the garbage when visiting our parents, they may be very impressed, thinking, "This is the first time in forty years my son has helped around the house. Buddhism is great!" The non-Buddhist wife of one of my students has supported and encouraged her husband for years to attend our annual nine-day retreat. Why? Because every time he returns from retreat he is calmer, communicates better, and is much more loving to his family.

Predicting which of our friends and family will be interested in the Dharma is difficult. We may assume a very dear friend will be interested, but he is not. Similarly, we may assume that a relative will not want to discuss Buddhist ideas only to discover that she is receptive. Therefore, while having our own agenda often alienates people, going along with our friend's level of interest and receptivity opens the door to good discussions.

How do we establish a daily meditation practice and what should it include?

Meditate in a clean, quiet place in your home, away from the telephone and computer. You can set up a small shrine there if you wish. Meditating at approximately the same time each day gets you into a good rhythm. The mind is fresh in the morning and many people find it easier to meditate then, before the activities of the day have begun. Other people prefer to meditate in the evenings. Make the meditation sessions a comfortable length, neither too short nor too long. You could start out with fifteen minutes and gradually extend it as you're able to sit longer.

Follow the instructions of your spiritual teacher on how to structure the sessions. You may start out with a few prayers to take refuge and set a good motivation for meditation. Then you could do some breathing meditation and, depending on your tradition, another type of meditation as well. Our meditation time is quiet time alone when we can digest our experiences, look at our lives, cultivate our good qualities, and enjoy our own company (and that of the Buddhas and bodhisattvas too!).

Must we go to the mountains and meditate to practice Dharma?

Not at all. Some people can happily remain in solitude and develop high realizations through meditation. But for a long retreat to be successful, we need to have accumulated great positive potential and to have a good foundation in the basic Dharma practices. These prerequisites can be gathered while living and practicing in society. In that way we integrate Dharma into our lives and simultaneously offer direct service to society. On the other hand, if we go to live in isolation with an emotional dream of becoming a great meditator when in fact we are unable to confront our dissatisfied mind, we'll return confused and unhappy. It's wiser to practice in a way that corresponds to our present mental state and ability.

How can we integrate Buddhism into our daily lives? How do we balance work and spiritual practice?

When you wake up in the morning, try to make your first thought, "Today, I don't want to harm anyone. I'm going to help others as much as possible. May all my actions be directed toward the long-term goal of becoming a Buddha to benefit others." After you get up, meditate for a while to get in touch with your inner calm, to learn about yourself, and to set a good motivation for the day.

During the day, be mindful of your feelings, thoughts, words, and actions. When you notice negative emotions or harmful behavior arising in yourself, apply the antidotes taught by the Buddha. For example, to counteract attachment, reflect on impermanence; and to subdue anger, contemplate patience, love, and the kindness of others. Of course, the more we have meditated on these previously, the easier it will be to recall and use them at the moment.

In the middle of a busy day, stop, breathe and get centered again before going on. Although this takes only a minute, it's sometimes hard to get ourselves to pause when we're on "automatic pilot." Pausing is a good habit to develop: instead of answering the phone right away, first think, "May I speak kindly and benefit the person on the line," and then pick up the phone. When we sit down at our desk, we can breathe quietly for a few seconds and then begin work. When we're stopped at a light or stuck in traffic, we can look around and think, "All these people around me want to be happy and to avoid problems just as I do. Because we live in an interdependent society, I receive benefit from the different jobs these people do, even though I don't know them personally." It's also very helpful to think like this when someone cuts us off! We can also have Dharma related reminders such as "compassion," "mindfulness," or *"om mani padme hum"* screen savers on our computer.

In the evening, take a little time to review the day's events, purify any harmful attitudes or behaviors, rejoice in the changes and positive attitudes you're developing, and dedicate all the positive potential for the enlightenment of all. We often expect "fast-food enlightenment," not wanting to expend much time or energy to gain it. Unfortunately, things don't work that way! Profound change occurs gradually. We need to rejoice at our own and others' development instead of being dissatisfied with what we haven't done.

What can we do if our practice weakens due to the influence of the external environment, and controlling our attachment becomes difficult?

Daily meditation practice is an excellent remedy. In the morning sit quietly and spend some time remembering the disadvantages of attachment, recalling impermanence and death, and generating loving-kindness toward others. During the day, be aware of what you think, say, and do. If we are strongly attached to something, it's best, as beginners, to keep some distance from it. Just as a compulsive eater on a diet has difficulty going to a dinner party and watching everyone else eat, so too we will find it difficult to be near objects of attachment and remain unaffected. As our internal practice gets stronger and we are less drawn to superficial "glitter," we can again be with those objects and people with a peaceful mind. If our friends encourage us to go to places or do things that make our previous habitual attachment, anger, or jealousy arise, we may suggest an alternative activity or decline the invitation. If we are sincere in our practice, we will naturally make new friends with a similar interest in Dharma, and they will encourage us to develop in a positive direction.

Chapter Fifteen

SOCIAL ACTIVISM AND ETHICAL ISSUES

What is the Buddhist attitude toward social welfare projects?

They are necessary and very good. As Buddhists, we try to develop love and compassion for others on a mental level, but this must be expressed in action as well. His Holiness the Dalai Lama has often commented that Buddhists can learn from the Christian example of active compassion through involvement in community welfare projects. Establishing schools, hospitals, hospices, counseling services, and food services for the needy directly benefits others. However, while engaging in this work, we must guard against partisanship, pride, and anger. Both our attitude and our actions must be directed toward benefiting others.

People have different dispositions and talents, and thus will practice the Dharma in various ways. Some will focus on study and teaching, others on work to benefit society, and others on meditation. Although not all Buddhists are inclined towards socially engaged projects, those who are can practice the Dharma in that context.

Does Buddhism condone social activism?

As with many questions, the answer begins with "It depends..." Depending upon our motivation and on the kind of changes we advocate and the methods we use, social activism may be helpful or harmful. Advocating policies or methods that run counter to the general Buddhist principles of nonviolence and tolerance is harmful. Even if we favor beneficial policies, if our motivation is askew, the long-term results will not be good. For example, an attitude of moral indignation that sees others in society as inept, manipulative, and selfish is scarcely a constructive motivation with which to engage in social action. If we frame a situation in terms of "us versus them," and claim our side is right because we care for the general welfare of society, while theirs is wrong, then our motivation is almost identical to theirs! Such an attitude leads us to despise the "other side," and again we are caught in the cycle of attachment to what is close to the self and hatred for what is opposed.

Social and political problems are neither clear-cut nor easily solved. Long-term vision and great effort are necessary. Although we know this intellectually, our words and actions sometimes indicate that we seek swift and simple solutions. We must try to develop compassion for all parties involved in a conflict because each of them wishes to be happy and to avoid problems. For example, if we regard loggers as destroyers of the environment and are concerned only with stopping their harmful activities, our outlook is limited. Loggers want happiness just as we do; they also have families to support. We must value their concerns and seek solutions that contain alternative means for them to earn a living.

Does the belief in future lives justify complacency in regards to social injustice? Does the law of karma indicate that we are to condone oppression? Does the wish for nirvana entail ignoring the ills of this world and seeking only the bliss of liberation?

No, to all three questions. People who do not have a good understanding of Buddhism may generate misconceptions such as: "Since rebirth exists, the poor will get another chance to be better off, therefore I don't need to help them now." "The oppressed must have created negative karma to experience such a result, and I'd be interfering with their karma if I tried to remedy their plight." "Suffering is inherent to cyclic existence. There's nothing that can be done, so I'll concern myself only with my spiritual practice, and disregard the world's ills." Such ideas reflect an incorrect understanding of karma and nirvana. Love and compassion for others are basic Buddhist principles, and acting according to them leads to liberation. The suffering in the world is due to karma, but we can still help stop or limit it. Although lasting happiness in cyclic existence isn't possible, we must still try to lessen gross suffering and bring relative happiness.

In fact, involvement in social action could be a means to lead others in the Dharma path. People certainly cannot meditate if they're hungry. Working to give them food stops their gross suffering and gives them contact with kind people. This may awaken their interest in spiritual practice.

On the one hand, no person is an island, and we need to reach out and help each other. On the other, meditation is a solitary pursuit that is necessary to develop wisdom and compassion. Must we choose between meditation and activity, or can they be balanced?

Both are important. Meditation enables us to purify our hindrances and to increase our good qualities so that when we reach out to others, we'll be effective. Just as a person who wants to cure others' illnesses studies in medical school before treating patients, a person who wishes to benefit others by showing them the Dharma path must study and practice before guiding others. Meditation provides the time and space to look within and to concentrate on developing good qualities and diminishing harmful ones. Activity in society gives us the opportunity to act according to the understandings we've developed through meditation. Interacting with others is like the "proof of the pudding," where what we still need to work on becomes clear. In addition, actively helping others enriches our mindstreams with positive potential so that our meditation can progress.

Because each of us is unique, we will balance these two things in different ways in our lives, and we may shift the balance between them from time to time, sometimes being more active, other times more contemplative. During the times we emphasize meditation, we must be careful that our altruism does not become abstract and intellectual. Similarly, while we're more active, we must meditate every day in order to retain a calm center from which to act.

How can we prevent burnout when we are working for others' welfare?

One way is to keep checking our motivation, continually renewing our compassionate intention. Another is to assess what we're capable of doing and to make realistic commitments. Sometimes we may be so inspired by the bodhisattva ideal that we agree to participate in every project that comes our way, even though we may lack the time or ability to complete it. As a result of over-commitment, we may push ourselves to the point of exhaustion or begin to resent those who are counting on our help. We should survey the situation and our capabilities well before we commit and accept only those responsibilities that we can carry out.

In addition, we must remember that difficulties and dissatisfaction are the nature of cyclic existence. Preventing nuclear waste, opposing oppression, stopping the destruction of rain forests, and helping the homeless are noble projects. However, even if all these goals were achieved, all the world's ills would still not be solved. The chief source of suffering lies in the mind. As long as ignorance, attachment, and anger are present in people's minds, there will be no lasting peace on the earth. Thus, expecting our social welfare work to go smoothly, becoming attached to the results of our efforts, or thinking, "if only this would happen, the problem would be solved" sets us up for discouragement when our aspirations are not actualized. We need to remember that in cyclic existence, there are better and worse states, but all are temporary and none bring ultimate freedom. If we are realistic, we can work in the world without expecting to bring about paradise on earth. And we can also follow our spiritual practice, knowing that it will ultimately lead to the cessation of our own and others' suffering.

Should we continue to try to help people who don't accept our help?

Each situation must be examined individually. First, we must check our motivation for helping others. Is it because we think we know what's best for "this poor person who cannot get his life together?"

Is it because we want to feel needed? If we have such attitudes, we're likely to try to force our advice on others, which will cause them to recoil.

We must also examine ourselves to discover if we've acted skillfully or if our help has undermined others' sense of self-esteem. In trying to help, have we left others feeling humiliated? Have we tried to fix their problem with the solution *we* consider best for them without consulting *them*? In such a case, our motivation may have been tainted with self-centeredness, even though we thought we were acting for others' benefit.

Sometimes we have acted in good faith and with skill, but others are unreceptive or even hostile to our efforts. In this situation, we should stop active help but still keep the door of communication open so that if they change later on, they'll feel comfortable contacting us. Stomping away from situations in which we've unsuccessfully tried to help and complaining, "See how much I've done for you and you don't appreciate it!" increases others' resentment and prevents them from seeking our aid in the future. Sometimes acceptance, patience, and inaction are the most effective ways we can be of aid.

Are Buddhists concerned about the environment?

They need to be! Unfortunately many people lack education on this subject. Even when environmental issues make the headlines, some Buddhists neglect to engage in simple acts, such as recycling, to protect the environment. Taking care to recycle our cans, jars, bottles, and paper is part of the practice of mindfulness in our homes! Compassion and concern for others should motivate us to minimize the use of disposable, nonrecyclable materials in temples and Dharma centers and to recycle the materials we can.

A significant number of Western and Asian Buddhists are concerned about the environment and are involved in socially engaged projects. The Buddhist Peace Fellowship (Box 4650, Berkeley CA 94704) is noteworthy and can supply reading lists, addresses of socially engaged Buddhist organizations worldwide, and back issues of their excellent journal. *The Path of Compassion*, edited by Fred

Eppsteiner and published by Parallax Press, provides a Buddhist perspective on social engagement.

Does Buddhism give guidelines for protection of the environment?

Yes. Interdependence, protecting life, and loving-kindness are three of the Buddha's most important teachings. Interdependence refers to the interrelationship of phenomena. In this case, sentient beings and the environment depend upon each other for survival, and thus it's in the interest of human beings to protect the environment. Traditionally, Buddhists advocate nonviolence and the protection of life. Because humans, animals, and insects are life-forms, Buddhism advocates the preservation of endangered species. In addition, as an expression of loving-kindness for ourselves, future generations, and all beings, Buddhism stresses the protection not only of the earth on which all of us depend, but also the protection of all sentient life on it.

Attachment is one of the chief causes of humankind's exploitation of the environment. Craving for more and better causes us to take all we can from the earth and to ignore the long-term consequences of this. If we lessen our attachment by developing contentment with what we have, we will be able to live more harmoniously with our environment and the other beings who share it with us.

What does Buddhism say about animal rights?

Buddhism regards animals as living beings who experience pleasure and pain and who cherish their own lives just as humans do. Therefore, Buddhists would not advocate putting homeless cats and dogs to sleep. Nor would they condone cruel experimentation on animals, the dreadful living conditions of animals raised for slaughter, or killing animals to have fur coats or sheepskin rugs. Although theoretically Buddhism favors vegetarianism, it is not required, and many Buddhists are not vegetarians.

Why do people in some Buddhist traditions eat meat, while those in others are vegetarian?

Initially, it may seem confusing that the Theravadins of Sri Lanka and Southeast Asia eat meat, the Chinese Mahayanaists do not, the

Japanese Mahayanaists do, and the Tibetans, who practice the Vajra-yana, do. This difference depends on the varying emphasis of each tradition: Theravadin teachings emphasize eliminating attachment toward sense objects and counteracting the discriminating mind that says, "I like this and not that." Thus, when the monastics collect alms, they are to accept silently and with gratitude whatever is offered to them, be it meat or not. If monastics said, "I cannot eat meat, so give me more of those delicious vegetables," the benefactors would be offended and the monastics' practice of nonattachment would be harmed. Thus, provided that the meat comes from an animal that the monastic neither kills himself, orders to be killed, nor sees, hears, or suspects is killed to provide him with meat, he is permitted to eat it. However, those who offer food to the sangha should remember that the principal premise of Buddhism is not to harm others and should choose what they offer accordingly.

Upon the basis of nonattachment, the Mahayana tradition emphasizes compassion for other beings. Thus, a practitioner of this tradition is advised not to eat meat in order to avoid inflicting pain on any being and to prevent potential butchers from committing negative actions. Also, the ignorant, lusty, or aggressive energy of an animal can affect an ordinary practitioner who eats its flesh, thus impeding his or her development of great compassion. Therefore, vegetarianism is recommended. The Chinese Mahayana monks and nuns are strict vegetarians while the laypeople may eat meat.

Although Japanese Buddhism is Mahayana, both the priests and the laypeople generally eat meat. This is due to the geography of Japan, where people have depended on the sea as a food source for centuries.

The tantric path, or Vajrayana, has four classes. In the two lower classes, external cleanliness and purity are emphasized as techniques to help the practitioner generate internal purity of mind. Therefore, these practitioners do not eat meat, which is regarded as impure. On the other hand, in the Highest Yoga Tantra, on the basis of nonattachment and compassion, a qualified practitioner employs the subtle nervous system in meditation. For this, one's bodily elements need to be very strong, and thus eating meat is recommended for such a person. Also, this class of tantra stresses the transformation of ordinary objects through meditation on selflessness. Such practitioners, by virtue of their profound meditation, are not greedily eating meat for their own pleasure.

In Tibet, an additional factor must be considered: due to the high altitude and harsh climate, there is little to eat besides ground barley, dairy products, and meat. The people had to eat meat to stay alive. However, His Holiness the Dalai Lama has encouraged the Tibetans living in exile in countries where vegetables and fruits are more plentiful to refrain from eating meat whenever possible.

If practitioners suffer severe health problems, their spiritual masters may encourage them to eat meat. In this way, they can keep their bodies healthy to use it for Dharma practice.

The Buddha prohibited all of his followers—ordained and lay—from eating meat under three circumstances: 1) when they kill the animal themselves, 2) when they ask another person to kill it for them, or 3) when they know or suspect that someone killed the animal to feed to them. By avoiding meat obtained in any of these three ways, people do not create the negative action of killing. The question then arises, "What about eating meat bought at the market?" Many teachers say that is permissible. My personal opinion is that some karma must be involved simply because consumer demand creates the supply of meat, which entails the taking of lives. However, this karma would be different from that created by directly killing the animal oneself.

If one does eat meat, eating the flesh of large animals is recommended. This minimizes the number of lives that are taken to provide a meal. Only one cow loses its life to provide many people with several meals, whereas many shrimp must die to give one person only one meal. People who eat meat are also encouraged to develop a sense of gratitude and compassion for the animals who have given their lives so they can eat. In this way, they will aspire to practice the Dharma well to repay the kindness of the animals. Also, non-vegetarians can recite the mantra *om ahbirakay tsara hung* seven times over the meat and pray for the animal to have a fortunate rebirth.

We cannot brand people as "good Buddhists" or "bad Buddhists" by looking at their dinner plates. Those who eat meat with a sense of gratitude and compassion for the animal may be more spiritual than "fundamentalist vegetarians" who are intolerant of anything but their own view. Each person must check his or her own level of practice, bodily requirements, and the food source in their environment and eat accordingly, without insisting that everyone else eat as he or she does. What we eat does not make us enlightened, but what we do with our minds does.

Is organ donation considered beneficial according to Buddhism?

In general, offering parts of one's body for the benefit of others is virtuous. Nowadays this is much easier than in the past because a kidney, for example, can frequently be transplanted from one person to another without great complications. However, each case must be regarded separately, depending on one's motivation and the other's condition.

Donating one's organs after death is a choice that will vary from person to person, depending on each individual's state of mind and level of spiritual practice. In some cases, removing organs after the heart has stopped but before the consciousness has left could interrupt the death process and be detrimental. In others, the force of the person's compassion and wish to benefit others can override any inconvenience that person may experience and could be an ultimate act of caring for others. This is a personal decision.

What is the Buddhist view on abortion?

According to Buddhism, the consciousness joins with the fertilized egg at the moment of conception, and thus the embryo is a living being. Unwanted pregnancy is a difficult situation, and we must think creatively about how to help people who face it. There is no black-and-white answer; each situation is unique. But no matter what choice is made, the pain cannot be denied.

Currently, a great debate rages in America about abortion, and both sides claim to be right. However, I see much anger and very little compassion in both camps. Nevertheless, compassion for the parents and the child involved in an unwanted pregnancy is what is needed. We must try to find the "best" solution in a case where no perfect solution exists, and we must consider both the short and long term effects on both the parents and the child. For example, abortion may terminate the pregnancy and solve the immediate problem, but the parents may have unresolved emotions afterward, and the karma they and the doctor create will adversely influence their future happiness.

Better education and counseling about birth control, especially for teenagers, are needed. Young people also need realistic education about romance. But to teach that, adults must first develop and model it themselves! And that means dismantling the conditioning from the fairy tales and Hollywood stories we grew up with. Also, we should improve adoption services to help the many childless couples have children. I appreciate the choice that the natural parents of my adopted relatives and friends made. Without it, I would never have known those people who are now very dear to me.

Is birth control allowed in Buddhism?

Yes, depending on the method. Birth control methods that prevent conception are permitted. However, once conception has taken place and consciousness has entered the fertilized egg, it's a different situation. Thus morning-after pills, IUDs, and other such methods are discouraged.

What is the Buddhist view on the death penalty?

Life is the most valuable possession any person has, even if that person acts in a criminal manner. Buddhism recommends rehabilitation or imprisonment rather than execution. The proper motivation is needed for imprisoning others, however. That is, imprisonment is to protect a person from harming others and from creating more negative karma that would bring him or her misery later. Seeking revenge or feeling glee at punishing others is opposite to the kind heart that Buddhism encourages us to develop.

Is self-defense ever justifiable in light of the Buddhist emphasis on nonviolence?

Self-defense does not need to involve violence, and nonviolence does not mean becoming a doormat. We can seek ways to protect ourselves from harm without harming others or by inflicting the least amount of harm necessary. With however much time is available, we can try to diminish our self-centeredness and reflect on compassion before acting.

Someone who cherishes others more than him or herself would generally choose to give up his or her own life rather than slay another. In ancient times a certain general was furious with a monk who refused to answer a question. Drawing his sword, the general shouted, "Do you know I could stick this into you without thinking twice?" The monk calmly replied, "And do you know I could have it stuck in me without thinking twice?" If we are unattached to our bodies and do not want to take the lives of others, we may be willing to give up our own lives.

However, most of us are not capable of doing that with a happy mind. If we feel we cannot avoid killing, we can at least try not to rejoice in the action, but do it with regret at having to cause another pain. If our intention to cause harm is weak, the karmic effect of the act will be less. Purification will also help diminish the strength of the karma.

What can we do in times of war or if someone threatens our loved ones?

Seeking nonviolent means to handle difficult situations is always better. If we use our intelligence and creativity, we can often find other solutions. Surely diplomacy is more effective than war. No matter how difficult our situation, we always have a choice of how to act. We can distract or injure someone rather than kill him or her. If there is a war, we should consider carefully what choice to make. We should weigh the advantages and disadvantages of killing and not killing in this and in future lives, and we should examine the effects this action has on ourselves and others. Then we can decide according to what we consider best (or least harmful!), although there may be no easy solution.

What can we do about insects in our house?

We can use creative ways to remove them! Killing them is not necessary. It may take a bit more time to put an ant on a piece of paper and carry it outside, or to catch a spider or cockroach in a plastic container and put it in the grass, but when we consider the consequences of killing and the fact that each insect cherishes its life just as we cherish ours, we won't mind the extra effort.

Is killing ever permissible?

In a story of one of Shakyamuni Buddha's previous lives as a bodhisattva, he was the captain of a ship. He knew that the oarsman was going to kill and rob the five hundred merchants on board. He had intense compassion not only for the victims, but also for the oarsman, who would experience the torturous karmic results of killing so many people. In addition, he was willing to take upon himself any negative karmic effects of killing. He thus decided to take the oarsman's life, but because his motivation was pure, the karmic effect of killing was minimal, and he created great positive potential that propelled him on the bodhisattva path.

Chapter Sixteen

WOMEN AND THE DHARMA

Can both men and women attain liberation and enlightenment?

Views on this differ among the various Buddhist traditions. According to the Vajrayana, both women and men are equally able to attain liberation and enlightenment. However, the Theravada and general Mahayana presentations say that although one can attain liberation with a female body, to attain full enlightenment one has to have a male body in the very last rebirth. As a Buddha, one is beyond being either male or female. An enlightened being can manifest in any type of body—human or animal, male or female—that is beneficial for sentient beings.

Our gender, like everything else, exists merely by being labeled. In this case, the label is designated in dependence on the cellular arrangement of our body. When we say, "I am female" or "I am male," that designation is based simply on the body we have this life time. In previous lives, each of us has been born male and female. When we watch our breath or observe our mind in meditation, we can clearly see that our mind is neither male nor female. In other words, there is nothing about us that is inherently male or female. Therefore, we should avoid making these labeled categories more solid than they actually are.

Can women make offerings and prayers during menstruation? Can they meditate at that time?

Of course! Any notion that they cannot is superstition.

Is it harder for a woman to practice the Dharma than for a man?

A general statement cannot be made, for each individual is different. Some women find that their menstrual cycle causes many emotional changes. But they can learn to deal with them. After all, men can be moody too! I believe that the principal thing holding a woman back is lack of self-confidence and a limited vision of her potential due to societal values or family upbringing. If we think we cannot do something well, we don't even try. What a waste of human potential! We are human beings with human intelligence, and have not only met the Dharma but also have all the necessary conditions to practice and attain realizations. So, let's do it! The success of our practice depends on our self-confidence and effort, not on others' opinions. Historically, many women have attained liberation and enlightenment. The *Therigatha,* some Mahayana sutras, and tantric biographies tell the stories of many female practitioners who became arhats, bodhisattvas, and Buddhas. Nowadays, too, we see women who are accomplished meditators, teachers, and leaders of Buddhist centers.

Have women participated as equals in Buddhist institutions?

In most Western and Asian cultures, women's activities have been more restricted and their social position lower than men's. The position and opportunities open to women in Western society have undergone much change in recent years, but haven't changed as much in Asia. In the sixth century B.C. when the Buddha was alive, women were considered subordinate to men, and their societal roles were very restricted. Conforming with Indian values, the Buddha designated that the nuns sit behind the monks and be served after them and that the nuns' community be under the care of the monks. This is due to the societal customs of ancient India, and is not indicative of women's intelligence or capability. In fact, while the male is representative of the method aspect of the path to enlightenment, the female is symbolic of the wisdom aspect!

Although it's said that the Buddha initially refused to admit women into the monastic order, he soon consented to the establishment of a nuns' community composed of fully-ordained women. These were revolutionary steps according to ancient Indian society. At that time, women were considered the property of first their fathers, then their husbands, and finally their sons. The Buddha's clear recognition of women's potential to attain liberation and enlightenment and his encouraging them in their practice by giving them full ordination was remarkable given the society in which he lived. Aside from the Jains, Buddhism was the only religion at that time to ordain women.

Although women's capability to practice the Dharma and attain high realizations has traditionally been recognized, women have occupied second place in Buddhist institutions due to cultural prejudice. However, internal practice is very different from external power and recognition. A true practitioner is more concerned with the former than the latter. That doesn't mean, however, that women must complacently accept institutionalized cultural biases. We must work to remedy them, motivated not by pride or anger, but because we want all beings—men and women alike—to be able to practice well and attain enlightenment.

In Buddhism, different levels of ordination exist for women— eight-precept holder, novice (sramanerika), probationary (siksamana), and fully-ordained nun (bhikshuni). The level of ordination available to women differs from one country to another, and this influences how various Asian societies regard their ordained female practitioners. In the Chinese, Korean, and Vietnamese traditions, women can take full ordination. Educated and active in society, many are spiritual masters themselves. In fact, Chinese nuns currently outnumber the monks. In contrast, the full ordination for women isn't available in Thailand, and the women who have taken eight precepts have an ambiguous status between lay and ordained. In Sri Lanka, women may take ten precepts and they have a similar ambiguous status. Among the Tibetans, the novice ordination for women is available, but the lineage of full ordination did not spread to Tibet. Although there have been several great female practitioners in Tibet, few Tibetan women currently teach the Dharma.

Women from Buddhist traditions that lack the lineage for women's full ordination are now interested in instituting this ordination in their tradition. Both monks and nuns are studying to determine how to transmit the ordination lineage from one tradition to another. Some women, both Asian and Western, have already gone to Taiwan, Hong Kong, France, or the U.S.A. to take the full ordination in Chinese, Vietnamese, or Korean temples.

What can be done to improve the situation of nuns and female practitioners?

As Buddhism comes to the West, cultural biases against women must and will be left behind because present Western cultures won't tolerate them. In addition, such prejudice is harmful to both men and women. At present in the West, women are very active in Buddhist organizations and often are leaders or teachers. However, because sexual discrimination still exists, we must be vigilant and ensure that biases against women don't creep into Buddhist translations, rituals, or education in the West. In particular, all translations of Buddhist texts and prayers should be gender neutral, using terms such as "Buddha's spiritual children" instead of "Buddha's sons" when referring to bodhisattvas.

New nunneries, nuns' communities, and educational institutions for women are being built in both Asia and the West. These need funds to operate and to help the Dharma flourish. Women who wish to do long retreats need support, as do those who organize social welfare programs, publish Dharma books, and translate texts. People could keep this in mind when they make offerings to support the Dharma.

Since 1987, international conferences for Buddhist women have been regularly held and Sakyadhita, an international Buddhist women's organization has been founded. At least two international newsletters for Buddhist women exist, and interest in improving all aspects of life for female practitioners is increasing. Seeing women from various cultures and traditions unite in their common aspiration to practice and actualize the Buddha's teachings is inspiring.

Chapter Seventeen

MONKS, NUNS, AND LAY PRACTITIONERS

What does taking ordination as a monk or nun entail?

Ordination involves taking certain precepts or vows established by the Buddha and making an effort to live according to them. It is founded upon a person's commitment to steer her or his physical, verbal, and mental energies in productive directions instead of indiscriminately acting out any thought that comes to mind. The novice ordination consists of taking ten precepts for life. These ten are subdivided into thirty-six in the Tibetan tradition. Full ordination involves taking over two or three hundred precepts, the number varying according to the Vinaya lineage and whether one is a man or woman.

Lay people can also take vows, in this case called the five lay precepts. These are to abandon killing, stealing, unwise sexual behavior, lying, and intoxicants. Some lay people may also take the eight precepts for life. The additional three are to abandon: 1) singing, dancing, playing music, and wearing ornaments, perfumes, and cosmetics; 2) sitting on a high or expensive seat or bed; and 3) eating after midday. When taking the eight precepts for life, the third precept is one of celibacy. In addition, a practitioner can take the eight precepts for just one day. This practice is commonly done on new and full moon days and on Buddhist festival days, although it may be done any day.

When people decide that they would like to become a monk or nun or to take the five lay precepts, they request their teacher to grant them ordination. If the teacher feels that they have a proper foundation, he or she will arrange the appropriate ceremony.

What are the benefits of taking ordination as a monk or nun? Is monastic ordination necessary to practice the Dharma?

Becoming a monk or nun is not necessary to practice the Dharma. Taking ordination is an individual choice that each person must make for him- or herself. Historically, many lay men and women have gained high realizations. It's inspiring to learn about their lives and to emulate them.

However, there are some advantages to being ordained: by living within the precepts, one is constantly accumulating positive potential. As long as ordained people aren't breaking the precepts, they are continuously enriching their mindstreams with positive potential even when they're asleep. They have more time for practice and encounter fewer distractions, because family obligations can consume much time and energy. Children require a lot of attention, and it's difficult to meditate if they are playing or crying nearby. People who see these things as distractions and who want to pacify their minds and accumulate a rich store of positive potential may decide to take ordination to have a more conducive situation for practice.

How can a lay person practice the Dharma?

Lay men and women can practice the Dharma in the same way as everyone else: by subduing their minds. In some Buddhist cultures, some people underestimate their potential by thinking, "I'm a lay person. Listening to teachings, chanting, and meditating are the work of monks and nuns. It's not my job. I just go to the temple, bow, make offerings and pray for the welfare of my family." While these activities are good, lay people are capable of a rich spiritual life, in terms of both learning Buddhism and integrating it into their daily life. Attending Dharma talks on a regular basis and retreats whenever possible is important. By doing this, people will understand the real truth and beauty of the Dharma. Otherwise, they will remain "joss stick Buddhists" (people who go to the temple and offer joss stick incense with much ceremony and little understanding), and if someone asks them a question about Buddhism, they'll have difficulty in responding. That is a sad situation. Nevertheless, many Buddhists in both Asia and the West are eager to meditate and study the Dharma, and this is a good sign.

Lay Buddhists can take the five lay precepts for the duration of their lives or take eight precepts on special days. In this way, they increase their practice of mindfulness as well as create much positive potential. In addition, they can attend weekend retreats and teachings at temples and Dharma centers or use some of their annual vacation time to go on longer retreats.

Responsibility for the existence and dissemination of the Buddha's teachings lies with the monks, nuns, and lay people. If we value the Buddha's teachings and want them to continue to exist and to flourish, we have the responsibility to learn and practice them ourselves according to our capabilities.

Do people become monks and nuns to escape the harsh realities of life?

Instead of "escaping" reality, sincere practitioners are trying to discover it! Chasing after sense pleasures, distracting ourselves by watching television, shopping, or drinking are ways of escaping reality, for these activities distract us from looking at the reality of death and the functioning of cause and effect. In the Dharma, this is seen as a form of laziness, because no effort is being made to subdue our attachment, anger, and closed-mindedness.

Those who ask this question think that having a job, a mortgage, and a family are difficult tasks and constitute the "harsh reality of life." But it is a much harsher reality to be honest with ourselves and to recognize our own mistaken conceptions and harmful behavior. People who meditate and pray may not be able to show a skyscraper or a paycheck as the sign of their success, but they are by no means lazy and irresponsible. Eliminating our anger, attachment, and closed-mindedness and changing our destructive physical, verbal, and emotional habits is hard work. Much effort over a long time is necessary to become a Buddha.

If people become monks or nuns thinking to have an "easy life," their motivation is impure and they will not find ordained life satisfying. The causes of suffering—attachment, ignorance, and anger—follow us everywhere. They don't need a passport to go with us to another country, nor are they left outside the monastery gates. If all we had to do to escape the hassles of life was to shave our head and put on robes, I think everyone would do it! But unfortunately, it's not that easy. As long as we have attachment, ignorance, and anger, we cannot escape problems whether we are ordained or not.

Some people think, "Only people who cannot make it in the 'real world' become monks and nuns. Maybe they have family problems, or they didn't do well in school, or they cannot get a good job. They live in the temple and take vows just to have a home and an occupation." Should people seek ordination for this reason, they lack the proper motivation, and the masters who give ordination need to weed such people out. On the contrary, those who take ordination with a correct motivation have strong aspiration to develop their potential, to subdue their minds, and to help others.

Do all monks and nuns take the vow to be celibate or may they marry?

All monks and nuns take a vow to be celibate. In Japan, the tradition of lay priests developed. These people do not take vows of celibacy and may marry. Some priests shave their heads and wear robes, others don't.

In Tibetan Buddhism, one may be a lay person with a family and still be a spiritual teacher. Out of respect for the Dharma, such teachers sometimes wear clothes that resemble monastic robes, but are not. This is sometimes confusing for people who cannot tell the difference in the clothes and wonder why a "monk" or "nun" has long hair. Thus, His Holiness the Dalai Lama asked these practitioners to add a white band to their shawls to indicate that they are lay, not monastic, practitioners.

Can someone be ordained for a short period of time, or must it be for one's entire life?

This differs in each Buddhist tradition. In Thailand, a man may become a monk for a few weeks or months and then return to lay life.

Most young men in Thailand do this, and it's considered an honor for his family. In the other traditions, monastic ordination is taken for life. However, if a person is unhappy being ordained and later wants to leave the order, he or she may return the vows and resume lay life. Some people choose to take the Eight Mahayana Precepts for a year, and their spiritual masters may give them permission to wear robes during this time, although they are technically still lay people.

What is the relationship between the sangha (monks and nuns) and lay practitioners?

As the Buddha designed it, the sangha's responsibility is to keep their vows, learn and practice the Dharma, and teach and guide the lay people. The lay people, in turn, provide the requisites for life—housing, clothes, food, and medicine. This system gave the ordained practitioners more time to study and meditate, so they could progress along the path and thus be able to guide others in society more effectively. This relationship has continued to some extent in all Buddhist traditions, although in various forms. In the Chinese Ch'an (Zen) tradition, work is valued as part of the practice, and monks and nuns tend the fields as well as study and meditate. In Thailand, the vow not to handle money is strictly kept, and the lay people not only provide everything the sangha needs, but also help with the manual work in the monasteries.

In Asia, monks and nuns are generally respected and cared for because those societies value Dharma practice. However, monastics should consider themselves the servants of others, and not become proud when they receive offerings or respect. If they do, their own practice will decline.

In the West the relationship between ordained and lay practitioners is still in its formative stages. It will be influenced by the democratic and less hierarchical nature of Western society. In some ways, this is beneficial, in others it is harmful. For example, the financial needs of Western ordained sangha are not always provided for by the monastery or center where they live. As a result, some Western monks and nuns are forced to don lay clothes and find jobs to support themselves. Others have enough to live hand to mouth, but if

they become ill, or want to travel to receive teachings or do long retreat, they face financial difficulties.

When people take ordination, do they reject their family and friends?

Not at all. Their deciding not to live a family life themselves does not
mean they reject their parents and siblings. Although monastics wish
to give up attachment to their family and friends, they still love their
family and appreciate their kindness. But they don't limit their affection to a comparatively small group of people. By extending their love
to include all others, ordained people seek to develop impartial love
for all beings and to consider them as part of their family. They reflect this by working to make the world a better place through their
religious practice.

By purifying and developing their minds, monastics are able to
guide others to lasting happiness through the Dharma. They know
this is of great benefit not only to their families but also to society as
a whole. Even if they do not attain high realizations in this lifetime,
they have a broad vision and work for long-range happiness and benefit. They think, "If I continue with my worldly life, my disturbing
attitudes will surface and I'll harm others as well as create the cause
for my own unfortunate rebirth. How can I help my family and all
others if that occurs? But if I practice the Dharma, my own abilities
will increase and I'll be able to help them better." In this way, their
hearts remain connected to their family and to all others, although
they do not live a family life as others do.

How should parents view their child's becoming a monk or nun?

They should be very happy. It's a sign that they have done a good
job as parents by instilling in their child a sense of ethical discipline
and care for others. Some parents become upset if their child wants
to become a monastic. They fear that he or she will not be happy or
will lack financial security. Some parents are angry, thinking, "We
paid so much for your education. Who will take care of us when
we're old if you're in a monastery?"

Parents with this attitude mean well and want their child to be happy. But having a family, career, and many possessions is not the only way to happiness. Of course, when Shakyamuni Buddha left his luxurious life at the palace to seek the lasting happiness of enlightenment, his parents were upset too! But parents who understand the Dharma will want their child to be happy now and in the future, and they will understand that religious practice is a way to bring that about. They'll rejoice that their child is devoting him or herself to the noble goals of the Dharma.

Is taking ordination a painful sacrifice?

It shouldn't be. Ordained people shouldn't feel, "I really want to do these things, but now I have vows and cannot." If they do feel this way, they won't be happy being ordained. Abandoning negative actions should be seen not as a burden but as a joy. Such an attitude comes from contemplating cause and effect.

When we take vows, whether they are the five precepts of a lay person or the vows of a monk or nun, we first generate the attitude, "In my heart, I really don't want to kill, steal, lie, and so on." Sometimes we may be weak in an actual situation and feel tempted to do these things. Taking precepts gives us extra strength and determination not to do what we really don't want to do. For example, we may sincerely want to abandon killing, but when cockroaches are in our flat, we may be tempted to use insecticide. Having taken the precept not to kill, we'll remember that we don't want to kill and will avert the disturbing attitudes that could cause us to act negatively. In this way, precepts are liberating, not confining, for they help us free ourselves from habitual, unwholesome tendencies.

Sometimes we encounter Buddhists, both lay and ordained, who are ill-natured and difficult to get along with despite their religious practice. Why is this so?

Not all Buddhists are already Buddhas! Some don't take the Buddha's guidance on ethical matters seriously. And even those who do must spend a long time transforming their minds. Dissolving anger isn't an easy process. We can understand this from our own experience. When we are in the habit of losing our temper, it takes more than just saying "I shouldn't do this" for us to stop. We must practice correctly and continuously in order to avoid falling back into familiar but dysfunctional emotions and behaviors. By training our minds over time, we will be able to channel our energy in different directions.

We have to be patient with ourselves, and similarly, we need to be patient with others. We're all fighting the same internal enemies—disturbing attitudes, negative emotions, and imprints of past actions. Sometimes we're strong in confronting them, other times we're carried away by anger, jealousy, attachment, or pride. It does no good to judge or blame ourselves when we succumb to our negative emotions. Likewise, blaming and criticizing others when they do so is fruitless. Knowing how difficult it is to transform ourselves, we must also be patient with others.

As practitioners of the same path, we must try to be harmonious and accept each others' weaknesses. Our job is not to point fingers and say, "Why don't you practice better? Why don't you control your temper?" Our job is to ask ourselves, "Why don't I practice better so their actions won't make me angry?" In addition, we must ask, "What can I do to help them?"

Although all practitioners aren't perfect, this doesn't mean the method taught by the Buddha is imperfect. Rather, this indicates that either these individuals do not practice it well or their practice is not yet strong enough. The Buddha's teachings, however, remain impeccable, and anyone who practices correctly and continuously will definitely be able to transform themselves and to attain high realizations.

Chapter Eighteen

SPIRITUAL TEACHERS

Is it necessary to have a spiritual teacher? How do we find one?

Having the guidance of one or more qualified spiritual mentors is very helpful. While books can give us information, a teacher is able to answer our questions and provide an example of how to integrate the teachings into our lives. We can have more than one teacher, although one of them usually becomes our principal, or root, teacher.

We are responsible for seeking qualified teachers. This is especially important given that there's such a spiritual supermarket in the West. Not everyone who teaches is a realized being, or even an ethical one. We must get to know teachers before accepting them as our teachers. To do this, we should attend teachings given by various people, observe their behavior, examine the quality of the teachings, and gradually decide.

What are qualities that we should look for in choosing a teacher?

Qualified teachers act ethically, have sound meditative experience, and correctly understand emptiness. They have also studied the Buddhist scriptures in depth, are able to teach a variety of Dharma subjects, and have a good relationship with their own teachers. They are motivated to teach out of genuine concern for their students, not out of desire for offerings and fame. They are compassionate and patient and will try to help their students no matter how many mistakes the students may make. They teach in accord with general Buddhist principles and do not alter the meaning of the Dharma in order to gain more students or receive more offerings.

Are all Dharma teachers monastics or can some be lay practitioners?

Dharma teachers may be either monastics or lay people. While lay teachers may have families, monastics are always celibate. In choosing teachers, we should see who sets a good example for us and follow those people.

How do we relate to our teachers?

We benefit from recognizing our teachers' good qualities and treating them with respect, because respecting others opens us to benefit from their guidance. Also, if we provide for our teachers and help them with tasks that need to be done, they will have more time to teach and we will gain invaluable experience and create positive potential. The most important element in relating to our teachers is to think about and put into practice the excellent teachings they give. Whether we receive Dharma instructions in a large group or privately, they are given to benefit us, and we should try to implement them as best we can.

Respecting our teachers and following their guidance doesn't mean allowing ourselves to get into unhealthy relationships with them. Some people talk about "surrendering" to the spiritual guide. What is to be surrendered is our egocentric disturbing attitudes and negative emotions, not our wisdom, common sense, and responsibility for our own lives. If a teacher tells us to do something that goes against general Buddhist principles, we should not to do it.

I have met women who were approached by spiritual teachers for sexual relationships. The women felt unsure of themselves or even guilty when they declined because they thought, "This is a high teacher. Maybe there are reasons for his behavior that I don't understand." Women should not doubt themselves. If they feel uncomfortable, they should say so directly and leave. Other women feel flattered that the teacher is paying attention to them and think they may have a special spiritual experience by having sexual relationships with him. Going along with this generally leads to disappointment and hurt and thus should be avoided.

In addition, doting on our teachers is inappropriate, as is being possessive of them and jealous of other students. Our teachers' role is to guide us to enlightenment, not to fulfill our emotional needs. Spiritual teachers are not substitutes for parents or therapists.

Sometimes our spiritual mentors may point out our faults. They do this out of compassion and to benefit us. At those times, we should examine ourselves and take the opportunity to learn about ourselves. Then, we should apply the Dharma teachings to our mind, modify our unproductive ways of thinking, and alter our bad behavior.

What can we think and do if we see a spiritual teacher or a monastic act in a way that seems inappropriate to us?

We must first develop a constructive attitude ourselves, and then determine a proper course of action. While whitewashing inappropriate behavior is not healthy, becoming indignant and raising a ruckus helps neither ourselves nor others. It's natural to feel disappointed when someone we respect acts in a way that seems unsuitable. But it's important to ask ourselves, "Am I disappointed and angry because that person isn't what I want them to be? Or am I sad because perhaps that person is having difficulties and needs help?" There's a big difference in the two attitudes. The first is self-centered—we are upset because someone we set up as an idol or role model isn't acting in the way we expect and want. The other is compassionate and seeks to benefit the person. We must examine our expectations and try to cultivate the latter attitude.

The next step is to think about how best to help in the situation. Each situation is different. In some cases, we can approach the person directly and ask about the behavior. In other situations, we may feel it's best to speak to the person's teacher or to their Dharma friends. Some situations can be resolved quietly, others may require public discussion. In any case, we should try to cultivate an attitude that is both honest and compassionate—not accusatory or self-righteous.

What is an appropriate title to use when addressing our spiritual mentors? What do the terms *lama, rinpoche, geshe, ajahn, roshi,* and *sensei* mean?

We may ask our teacher how they prefer to be addressed. Monastics are generally called "venerable," although some use the terms "sister" or "brother." "Ajahn" is a term used in the Theravada tradition indicating someone who is a teacher or a senior monastic. "Sensei" and "roshi" are used in the Japanese Zen tradition, the former meaning "teacher" and the latter indicating a certain level of accomplishment in practice. "Lama," "rinpoche," and "geshe" are found in the Tibetan tradition. "Lama" may be used under a variety of circumstances. It means "teacher," (*guru* in Sanskrit) and is used for highly respected masters. Other times it indicates having done a three-year meditation retreat. "Rinpoche" may indicate a recognized reincarnation of a spiritual master, or it may be used as a term of respect for one's own teacher. "Geshe" is an educational degree, comparable to a Ph.D. in Buddhism.

It is easy to get lost in titles and to confuse titles with actual accomplishments. In addition, some people like titles and use many of them although their spiritual accomplishments are few, while others are more modest and refuse to use titles even though they have deep knowledge and experience of the Buddha's teachings. We should never rely on someone's titles, but should check their knowledge and personal qualities before establishing a student-teacher relationship with them.

Chapter Nineteen

FAMILY AND CHILDREN

What does Buddhism say about romantic love and marriage?

Romantic love is generally plagued with attachment, which is why many marriages end in divorce. When people fall in love with an image they created of the person, instead of with the actual human being, false expectations proliferate. For example, many people in the West unrealistically expect their partner to meet all of their emotional needs. If someone came up to us and said, "I expect you to always be sensitive to me, continuously support me, understand me no matter what I do, and meet all my emotional needs," what would we say? Undoubtedly, we would tell them that we are one limited being, they had the wrong person! In a similar way, we should avoid having such unrealistic expectations of our partners.

Each person has a variety of interests and emotional needs. Therefore, we need a variety of friends and relatives to share and communicate with. Nowadays, because people move so often, we may need to work harder to develop several stable, long-term friendships, but doing so strengthens our primary relationship.

For a romantic relationship to survive, more than romantic love is needed. We need to love the other person as a human being and as a friend. The sexual attraction that feeds romantic love is an insufficient basis on which to establish a long-term relationship. Deeper care and affection, as well as responsibility and trust, must be cultivated.

In addition, we do not fully understand ourselves and are a mystery to ourselves. Needless to say, other people are even more of a mystery to us. Therefore, we should never presuppose, with a bored attitude that craves excitement, that we know everything about our partner because we have been together so long. If we have the awareness of the other person being a mystery, we will continue to pay attention and be interested in him or her. Such interest is one key to a long-lasting relationship.

How can Buddhism help our family life?

Family harmony is extremely important, and divorce is traumatic for adults and children alike. If adults see the main purpose of marriage as pleasure, then arguments and the breakup of the family come about more easily. As soon as people don't get as much pleasure as they want, discontent sets in, quarrels ensue and the marriage collapses. Many people go on to have numerous partners, but still fail to find satisfaction. This is a clear example of the way in which clinging to one's own pleasure brings pain to oneself and others.

If both partners hold the Dharma as the center of their relationship, their relationship will be more satisfying. That is, both partners are determined to live ethically and to develop their loving-kindness toward all beings impartially. Then they will support each other to grow and to practice. For example, when one partner becomes discouraged or starts to neglect Dharma practice, the other can help him or her get back on track through gentle encouragement and open discussion. If the couple has children, they can arrange for each other to have time for quiet reflection as well as time with the children.

Although raising children is time-intensive, parents should not see this as antithetical to Dharma practice. They can learn a lot about themselves from their children and they can help each other work through the challenges of parenthood in the light of Buddhist values.

Influenced by contemporary trends in psychology, many people have come to attribute most of their problems to childhood experiences. However, if this is done with an attitude of blame— "I have problems because of what my parents did when I was a child"—it sets the stage for them to feel guilty and fearful that they will damage their own children when they have families. This kind of anxiety is scarcely conducive to healthy child-rearing or to feeling compassion for ourselves. Viewing our childhood as if it were an illness that we have to recover from only damages us as well as our children.

Although we cannot ignore detrimental influences from childhood, it's just as important to pay attention to the kindness and benefit we have received from our families. No matter what our situation was when we were growing up, we were the recipients of much kindness from others. Remembering this, we allow ourselves to feel the gratitude that naturally arises for those who have helped us. If we do, we also can pass that same kindness and care on to our children.

How can the Dharma help children? How can we teach the Dharma to children?

The essence of the Buddha's teaching is to avoid harming others and to help them as much as possible. These are values that both Buddhist and non-Buddhist parents want to instill in their children so that they can live harmoniously with others. Since children learn largely through example, the most effective way for parents to teach their children good values is to live them themselves. Of course, this isn't always so easy! But if parents try to practice well, their children will directly benefit from their example.

Growing up with Buddhism in the home helps children. If a family has a shrine, the children can keep it tidy and make offerings. One friend and her three-year-old daughter bow to the Buddha three times every morning. The child then gives the Buddha a present—some fruit or cookies—and the Buddha gives one back to the child (usually the previous day's offering). The little girl loves this ritual. Children like music, and the melodies of prayers, mantras, and Buddhist songs can take the place of the usual commercial jingles and nursery rhymes. Many parents chant mantras to their babies when the infants are upset or sleepy, and the babies react positively to the gentle vibration. In another family I know, the five-year-old son leads the prayer when they offer their food before eating. These are simple yet profound ways for parents and children to share spirituality.

Several Buddhist families could gather together on a weekly or monthly basis to practice together. Rather than just taking the kids to Sunday School and letting someone else teach them, practicing together provides the opportunity for the parents and children to spend some peaceful time together apart from their harried schedules. It also enables Buddhist families to meet and support each other. Activities for young children could include singing Buddhist songs, prayers, and mantras, learning to bow to the Buddha and make offerings at the shrine, and doing a short breathing meditation. Parents and school-age children could role-play together, creating a scene in which all the characters think of their own happiness above others' and then replaying it with one of the characters thinking of others' happiness. Such activities teach children problem-solving and let them see the results of different behaviors. Families could also visit Buddhist temples and centers in the community together.

Reading Buddhist children's books and watching Buddhist videos are other activities parents can share with their children. There is an excellent cartoon video of the Buddha's life, and many children's Dharma books. Informal discussions with children can be both amusing and instructive, and parents may be surprised how open their children are to concepts such as rebirth, karma, and kindness to animals.

Many parents exclaim, "My child can't sit still!" My guess is that these children have seldom seen their parents sit peacefully either! When children see an adult sitting peacefully, they get the idea that they can as well. Sometimes a parent's quiet time can be shared with their children. For example, a child can sit on his or her parent's lap while the parent recites mantras. Other times, parents may want to be undisturbed when they meditate, and children learn to respect their parents' wish for quiet time.

Discussion groups work well with teenagers. An adult can facilitate a discussion about friendship or other topics of concern to teenagers. The beauty of Buddhism is that its principles can apply to every aspect of life. The more children see the relevance of ethical values and loving-kindness to their lives, the more they will value those traits. Once I led a discussion group for twenty teenagers about boy-girl relationships. Each person spoke in turn, and although they were ostensibly talking about their lives and feelings, there was a lot of Dharma in what they said. For example, they brought out the importance of living ethically. As the facilitator, I didn't teach or preach. I just listened and respected what they said. Afterward some of them came up to me and said, "Wow! That's the first time we've ever talked about that with a nun!" Not only were they able to talk openly in the presence of an adult about a sensitive topic, but they also understood that religious people are aware and sympathetic of teenagers' concerns. In addition, they saw the relevance to their lives.

What if our children aren't interested in Buddhism? Should we allow them to go to church with their friends?

Religion should not be forced on anyone. If children aren't interested in Buddhism, let them be. They can still learn how to be a kind person from observing their parents' attitudes and actions.

Classmates are likely to invite their friends to go to church with them. Because we live in a multicultural and multireligious society, it's helpful for children to learn about other traditions by attending their friends' church or temple. When they do so, we should prepare them by discussing the fact that people have different beliefs, and thus mutual respect and tolerance are important. Our children can also invite their classmates to a Dharma center or Buddhist activities, thus promoting mutual learning and respect.

How can we introduce children to meditation?

Children are often curious when they see their parents do their daily meditation practice. This can be an opportunity to teach them a simple breathing meditation. Children enjoy sitting quietly alongside their parents for five or ten minutes. When their attention span sags, they can quietly get up and go in another room while the parents continue to meditate. If parents find this too disturbing, they can do their daily practice privately and meditate together with their youngsters at another time.

Children can also learn visualization meditation. Most children love to pretend and can easily imagine things. Parents can teach their children to imagine the Buddha, made of light. Then, while light radiates from the Buddha into them and all the beings around them, they can chant the Buddha's mantra. If a child has a sick relative, friend, or pet, or if a friend is having problems, the child could visualize that person specifically and imagine the Buddha sending light to him or her. In that way, children increase their compassion and feel involved in helping those they care about.

Dharma centers usually schedule events for adults and no child care is provided. What can we do?

Dharma centers need to gradually expand their range of activities. Parents who are members could meet together and discuss how to do this, utilizing some of the suggestions above. They then can organize family activities or activities for children at the centers.

How can we have good relationships with our children, especially when they're teenagers?

Having an open relationship with teenagers is important, and this depends on how the parents relate to their children when they're small. This, in turn, depends on spending time with the children and on having a positive attitude toward them. When parents are harried, they tend to see having children as a hassle—yet another thing to take care of before they collapse after a hard day at work. Children pick up on this, often feeling that their parents don't care about them or don't have time for them even if they care. Setting priorities is essential in building good relationships with children. This may mean accepting a job that pays less but has shorter hours or turning down a promotion that would have increased family income but meant more stress and less time at home. Love is more important to children than material possessions. Choosing to earn more money at the expense of good family relations may mean later having to spend that extra income on therapy and counseling for both parents and children!

Do children need discipline? How do we do that without getting angry?

Children often provide the best—and the most difficult—opportunity to practice patience! For that reason, parents are advised to become familiar with the antidotes to anger that the Buddha taught. Patience doesn't mean letting children do whatever they want to. That is, in fact, being cruel to children, for it allows them to develop bad habits, which makes it more difficult for them to get along with others. Children need guidelines and limits. They need to learn the results of different behaviors, and how to discriminate between which to practice and which to abandon.

Contentment is an essential Buddhist principle. How can we teach it to children?

The attitude of contentment enables us to enjoy life more and experience more satisfaction. I believe one reason children are discontent is that they are given too many choices about their sense pleasures. From a young age, they are asked, "Do you want apple juice or orange juice?" "Do you want to watch this TV show or that one?" "Do you want this kind of bicycle or that?" "Do you want a red toy or a green one?" Children—not to mention adults—become confused by being bombarded with so many choices. Instead of learning to be content with whatever they have, they are constantly forced to think, "Which thing will bring me the most happiness? What else can I get to make me happy?" This increases their greed and confusion. Remedying this doesn't mean that parents become authoritarian. Rather, they place less emphasis on the importance of these things in the home. Of course, this also depends on parents' altering the ways they themselves relate to sense pleasures and material possessions. If parents cultivate contentment, their children will find it easier to do so as well.

Chapter Twenty

SHRINES AND OFFERINGS

What is the purpose of a shrine? What is put on it?

People often like to set up a simple shrine in their homes in a clean, quiet place. Images of the Buddhas, Buddhist deities, and bodhisattvas are placed on a shrine as a symbol of the Buddhas' enlightened physical forms. Those following Tibetan Buddhism put photos of their spiritual teachers above these, but people from other Buddhist traditions don't necessarily do this. To the Buddha's right (the left side of the shrine as we look at it) is a text, representing the Buddha's enlightened speech. To the Buddha's left is a bell or a stupa (relic monument), symbolizing the Buddhas' enlightened mind. Various offerings are placed in front of these.

The figures on a shrine reminds us of the good qualities of the Buddhas, Dharma, and Sangha, thus inspiring us to develop those same good qualities. Some days we may feel agitated, angry, or depressed. When we pass by a shrine in our homes or visit a temple and see the photos of our spiritual mentors or the peaceful figure of the Buddha, it helps us remember that there are beings who are peaceful and we can become like them. Automatically, our minds settle down.

Do Buddhists worship idols?

Not at all! A piece of clay, bronze, or jade is not the object of our respect and worship. For example, if we go to a place far away from our family, we're likely to take a photo of them with us to remember them better. When we look at the photo and feel love for our family, we are not loving the paper and ink of the photo! The photo merely strengthens our memory. It is similar with a statue or painting of the Buddha.

When bowing before images of the Buddha, we recall the qualities of the enlightened beings and develop respect for their impartial love and compassion, generosity, ethical conduct, patience, joyous effort, concentration, and wisdom. The statue or painting reminds us of the qualities of the Buddhas, and we bow to those qualities, not to the clay. In fact, having a figure of the Buddha to bow before is not necessary. We can remember the Buddhas' qualities and develop respect without it.

Showing respect to the Buddhas and their qualities inspires us to develop these extraordinary qualities ourselves. We become like the people we respect, so when we take the loving-kindness and wisdom of the Buddhas as our example, we strive to become like them.

What is the purpose of making offerings to the Buddhas?

We don't make offerings because the Buddhas need them. When someone has purified all defilements and enjoys the bliss that comes from wisdom, he or she certainly doesn't need an apple or an incense stick to be happy! Nor do we make offerings to win the Buddhas' favor. The Buddhas developed impartial love and compassion long ago and won't be swayed by flattery and bribery the way ordinary beings are!

Making offerings helps us create positive potential and develop our good qualities. At present, we have excessive attachment and miserliness. We tend to keep the biggest and best for ourselves and give the second best or something we don't want to others. But these self-centered attitudes make us feel consistently poor and dissatisfied no matter how much we have. In addition, we fear losing what little we do have. Such attitudes make us restless and lead us to act dishonestly to get more things or to be unkind to others to protect what we have.

One purpose of making offerings is to pacify these harmful emotions of attachment and miserliness. Thus, when making an offering, we try to do so without any feelings of loss or regret. Water is readily accessible so that we can easily offer it without attachment or miserliness, bowls of water are often offered on the shrine. By offering with a happy mind, we habituate ourselves to the thought and action of giving. Thus, we come to feel rich when we give and take pleasure in sharing good things with others.

Some people wonder if the Buddhas actually receive the offerings. A cute story tells of a young monk staying up late to see if the Buddha image in the prayer hall took the offerings in the middle of the night. Don't think that the Buddhas don't receive the offerings just because the flowers and fruit are still on the shrine the next day. They can receive them, enjoying the essence of the offerings, without taking them away.

Since the Buddhas, bodhisattvas, and arhats are the highest of all beings, making offerings to them has special meaning. We usually give gifts to our friends because we like them. Here, we make offerings to the holy beings because we are attracted to their qualities. We shouldn't make offerings with the intention to bribe the Buddhas: "I offered you incense, now you are obliged to grant my prayers!" Rather we practice giving with a respectful and kind attitude. If we later make a request, we do so with humility.

What is offered on the shrine?

Anything we consider beautiful can be offered. Traditional offerings are water, flowers, incense, light, perfume, and food, but we can offer other things as well. Those in the Tibetan tradition generally offer seven bowls of water each morning. The water is removed at the end of the day and thrown in a clean place or sprinkled over flowers and plants, while the empty bowls are placed upside down. Food that is offered should be removed from the shrine before it spoils. We may eat it or give it to others, although food that has been offered on the shrine isn't generally fed to animals.

Is there a symbolic meaning to each offering?

Yes. Flowers represent the qualities of the Buddhas and bodhisattvas, incense the fragrance of pure ethics. Light symbolizes wisdom, and perfume represents confidence in the holy beings. Offering food is like offering the nourishment of meditative concentration, and music symbolizes impermanence and the empty nature of all phenomena.

While we may physically offer one flower, mentally we can imagine the entire sky filled with beautiful flowers and offer these as well. Imagining lovely things and then offering them to the Buddhas and bodhisattvas enriches our mind. Similarly, we can offer things mentally without placing them on the shrine. For example, when we see beautiful things in showcase windows or witness the loveliness of nature, we can mentally offer these to the Three Jewels. This helps us avoid attachment to these things.

Do Buddhists say grace before eating?

Yes, there is the practice of offering our food before eating. Usually we dive into a plate of food with great attachment, little mindfulness, and even less real enjoyment. Instead, we can pause before eating and reflect on our motivation. Here we think that we are not eating for temporary pleasure or to make our body attractive. Rather, we eat to keep our body healthy so that we can practice the Dharma and benefit all beings. Reflecting on the kindness of those who planted, harvested, transported, and packaged our food, we feel interconnected with them and want to repay their kindness by using the occasion of eating to create positive potential for their benefit. For this reason, we offer the food.

Imagine the food as blissful nectar and offer it to a small Buddha made of light in our heart center (chakra). This Buddha represents all the enlightened beings combined with our own Buddha potential. The Buddha enjoys the nectar and radiates light that fills our entire body and makes us very blissful. In this way, we remain mindful of the Buddha as well as of the process of eating. We create positive potential by making offerings to the Buddha, and we also enjoy the food more. Before eating, some people like to recite the verses:

> To the supreme teacher, the precious Buddha; to the supreme practice, the holy precious Dharma; to the supreme guides, the precious Sangha; to all the objects of refuge, we make this offering.

May we and all those around us never be separated from the Triple Gem in any of our lives. May we always have the opportunity to make offerings to them. And may we continuously receive their blessings and inspiration to progress along the path.

If you are alone or eating with Dharma friends, you may want to pause before eating to do the reflection and visualization and to recite the verses. If you are in a restaurant or with people who are not Buddhist, you don't need to make a display of offering your food. Instead, simply do the reflection, visualization, and offering mentally while the others are getting settled or chatting.

Chapter Twenty-one

PRAYER, RITUAL, AND DEDICATING POSITIVE POTENTIAL

What is the role of prayer? Can prayers be answered?

There are many kinds of prayers. Some are designed to direct our minds toward a certain spiritual quality or aim, inspiring our mind to work to develop it and thus creating the cause for us to attain this. An example is praying to be more tolerant and compassionate toward others. Other prayers are for specific people or situations, for example praying for a person's illness to be cured or for that person's mind to be peaceful and his life meaningful in spite of the illness.

For any prayer to be fulfilled, prayer alone isn't sufficient. The appropriate causes must also be created. We can't simply think, "Please, Buddha, make this and that happen. I'll relax and have tea while you do the work!" For example, if we pray to be more loving and compassionate and yet make no effort to control our anger, we aren't creating the cause for that prayer to be fulfilled. The transformation of our minds comes from our own effort, but we can pray for the Buddhas' inspiration to do so.

Receiving the blessings of the Buddhas doesn't mean that something tangible comes from the Buddha and goes into us. It means that our minds are transformed through the combined effort of the teachings, the guidance of the Buddhas and bodhisattvas, and our own practice. "Requesting the Buddhas' blessings" has the connotation of requesting to be inspired by them so that our minds and actions are transformed and become more beneficial.

Some Buddhist practitioners seek to be born in a pure land in their next life because all the conditions there are conducive for Dharma practice and developing wisdom and compassion are comparatively easy. But we cannot pray to be born in a pure land and expect the Buddhas and bodhisattvas to make it happen! We must also make effort to actualize the teachings by not selfishly clinging to worldly pleasures and by generating compassion and an understanding of emptiness. If we do our part, then praying will have a profound effect on our minds. On the other hand, if we make no attempt to correct our harmful habits and if our minds are distracted while we pray, the effect is minimal.

Some people pray for another's sickness to be cured, for the family finances to improve, or for a deceased relative to have a good rebirth. For these things to occur, the other people involved must have created the necessary causes. If they have, our prayers provide the condition for the seed of constructive actions they did in the past to ripen into that result. However, if they haven't created the causal seeds through their own positive past actions, it's difficult for our prayers to be fulfilled. We can put fertilizer and water on the ground, but if the farmer hasn't planted the seed, nothing will grow.

When the Buddha described the working of cause and effect in our mindstreams, he said that killing causes us to have short lives or much illness. Abandoning killing and saving the lives of others causes us to have a long life, free from illness. If we neglect to follow this basic advice and yet pray for a long and healthy life, we have missed the point! On the other hand, if we abandon killing and save lives, prayers can help those positive seeds to ripen.

In addition, the Buddha said generosity is the cause of wealth. If we have been generous in a past life and now pray for our wealth to increase, our finances could improve. Yet, if we are miserly now, we are creating the cause for poverty, not wealth, in the future. In this case, no matter how much we pray to be financially comfortable, our actions are creating the cause for the opposite result. Instead we need to cultivate generosity—helping those in need and sharing what we have.

What is the purpose of rituals? Are they necessary?

Rituals are designed to help us counteract our disturbing attitudes and destructive actions and to develop our good qualities and positive actions. Rituals are a means, not an end in themselves. Because we are beginners and often have difficulty in distinguishing what to practice and what to abandon on the path, prayers written by advanced practitioners give us guidelines to follow. Saying the prayers can help us tune into the meanings they express. While we read or recite them, we should simultaneously try to meditate and transform our minds into the mental states described in the rituals. When we do a ritual alone, we can pause to concentrate on particular points that touch us deeply.

We do not need to limit our prayers to those composed by other people. As we study the Dharma and become familiar with the path to enlightenment, prayers may spontaneously arise in our minds. Events that evoke prayers may occur in our lives, and these can be very helpful in deepening our experience of the Dharma.

Some people like rituals and find them useful for their practice. Other people find them distracting. A person may want to do more rituals at certain times and fewer at others. Everyone is unique, and there are no hard and fast rules. We must do what feels comfortable to us and not do rituals simply because everyone else is doing them.

What are some common Buddhist rituals?

Rituals found in all Buddhist traditions include turning for refuge to the Buddha, Dharma, and Sangha, taking precepts to avoid harmful behavior, praising the qualities of the Three Jewels, making offerings to them, generating loving-kindness toward others, revealing our own mistakes, and rejoicing in the happiness and good qualities of others. In addition to these, each tradition has unique prayers reflecting those aspects of the path it emphasizes.

What role does chanting play in our spiritual development?

Chanting can be very beneficial if done with a proper motivation such as to prepare for future lives, attain liberation from cyclic existence, or become a Buddha to benefit others most effectively. For chanting to be effective in generating positive states of mind, we must try to concentrate and reflect upon the meaning of what we chant. Chanting profound prayers with a mind distracted by thoughts of food or work or parties has little effect. A tape recorder could also chant the names of the Buddha and say prayers! But if we transform our thoughts so they correspond to what we're chanting, then chanting becomes very powerful and beneficial.

A complete spiritual practice includes more than chanting. Listening to teachings, contemplating and discussing their meaning, and integrating them into our daily life enables us to think, feel, speak, and act in beneficial ways. Chanting alone cannot liberate us from cyclic existence. Deep meditation is necessary to generate the wisdom realizing selflessness.

What is the difference between a prayer and a mantra? Is it necessary to chant them in a foreign language that we don't understand?

Mantras are prescribed syllables to protect the mind. We want to protect our minds from attachment, anger, ignorance, and so on. Sometimes we seem to have an endless flow of internal chatter, with our mind making comments about what this person is wearing and what that person said. Reciting mantras is a skillful way to transform this tendency for internal chatter so that instead of commenting on useless, trivial things, we focus our mind on reciting syllables spoken by a Buddha. When combined with the four opponent powers (explained in the chapter on karma), mantra recitation acts as a powerful antidote that purifies negative karmic imprints on our mindstreams. While reciting mantras, we train our minds to think, feel, and visualize in beneficial ways, thus building up constructive mental and emotional habits. In addition, recitation of mantras calms our mind and heightens our concentration.

Mantras are recited in Sanskrit, rather than being translated into other languages, because they are the words spoken by a Buddha while in a deep state of meditation. The sound of these syllables can induce beneficial energy or vibration. While reciting a mantra, we can concentrate on the sound of the mantra, on its meaning, or on the accompanying visualizations that our spiritual mentor has taught us.

Prayers, on the other hand, were composed by great spiritual masters to help us develop constructive attitudes. They did this because sometimes we have difficulty differentiating between which attitudes and actions to practice and which to abandon in our Dharma practice. Prayers express the essence of constructive mental states, and when we think about the meaning of the prayers, our minds are transformed into those attitudes. Because understanding the meaning of the prayers is important, they can be translated from one language to another. Although chanting prayers in Asian languages can be quite lovely and inspiring, we can also do them in our own language because this facilitates our understanding.

What does the mantra *om mani padme hum* mean?

Om mani padme hum is the mantra of the Buddha of Compassion, Avalokiteshvara (Kuan Yin, Kannon, Chenresig). The meaning of the entire path to enlightenment is contained in the six syllables of this mantra. *Om* refers to the body, speech, and mind of the Buddhas, which is what we want to attain by our practice. *Mani* means jewel and refers to all the method aspects of the path—the determination to be free from cyclic existence, compassion, generosity, ethics, patience, joyous effort, and so on. *Padme* (pronounced "pay may" by the Tibetans) means lotus and refers to the wisdom aspect of the path. By uniting both method and wisdom in a combined practice, we can purify our mindstreams of all defilements and develop all of our potentials. *Hum* (sometimes written *hung*) refers to the mind of all the Buddhas.

Recitation of *om mani padme hum* is very effective for purifying the mind and developing compassion. We may recite it out loud or silently, and at any time. For example, if we are waiting in a queue, instead of getting impatient and angry, we can mentally recite this mantra and generate compassionate thoughts for those around us.

There is the custom of giving an oral transmission of a mantra, which means a spiritual teacher recites it and we either listen or repeat it after him or her. This transmits to us the energy of the lineage of practitioners who have used this mantra, and it makes our recitation of the mantra more powerful. However, even without receiving the oral transmission of *om mani padme hum* we may recite it and receive benefit from its calming energy.

What is merit? Isn't it selfish to do positive actions just to get merit, as if it were spiritual money?

The English word "merit" doesn't convey the Buddhist connotation, because it reminds us of getting gold stars in school and being rewarded because we did well. That is not the meaning intended here, and therefore "positive potential" is a better translation of the Buddhist word. No one is rewarding us when we act constructively. Rather, we leave positive imprints, or seeds, on our mindstreams, and when the necessary cooperative conditions are present, they will bear fruit. This isn't a physical seed or imprint, but an intangible one, a positive potential.

Grasping at positive potential as if it were spiritual money is neither proper nor beneficial. If we do so, we are likely to quarrel with other people over who can make offerings first or become jealous of others because they do more virtuous actions than we do. Such attitudes are certainly not beneficial! While we should take advantage of opportunities to create positive potential, we must do so to improve ourselves, to create the causes for happiness, and to help others, and not out of attachment or jealousy.

Why must positive potential be dedicated? What should it be dedicated for?

Dedicating our positive potential is important in order to prevent it from being destroyed by our anger or wrong views. Just as a steering wheel guides a car, dedication guides how our positive potential ripens. Dedicating for the most extensive and noble goals is best. If we do so, all the lesser results will naturally come. If we dedicate our positive potential, however small, toward the ultimate happiness and enlightenment of all sentient beings, this automatically includes dedicating for a good rebirth and for the happiness of our relatives and friends.

Some people think, "I have so little positive potential. If I dedicate it for the happiness of everyone, then I won't have any left for myself." This is incorrect. Dedicating our positive potential to others doesn't deprive us of its benefits. Rather, it expands the field of those who will receive benefit from our actions. While dedicating our positive potential for the benefit of all beings, we can still make special prayers for the happiness of particular people who are undergoing difficulties at that time.

Can merit be transferred to deceased relatives or friends?

"Dedicating" positive potential (merit) rather than "transferring" it conveys the meaning better. We cannot transfer positive potential the way we can transfer the title to a piece of property or the way I can give you my car because you don't have one. Those who create the causes are the ones who experience the results. I cannot create the cause and have you experience the result, because the imprint or seed of the action has been implanted on my mindstream, not yours. So if our deceased relatives and friends didn't act constructively while they were alive, we cannot create good karma and then give it to them.

However, our prayers and offerings on their behalf can create the circumstances necessary for a positive action they created to bear fruit. A seed planted in a field needs the cooperative conditions of sunshine, water, and fertilizer to grow. Likewise, a seed or imprint of an action will ripen when all the cooperative conditions are present. If the deceased have done beneficial actions while they were alive, the additional positive potential we create by making offerings or engaging in virtuous actions—reciting and reading Dharma texts, making statues of the Buddha, contemplating love and compassion for all beings, and so forth—can help them. We can dedicate the positive potential from these actions for the benefit of the deceased, and this could help their own virtuous seeds to ripen.

GLOSSARY

Altruistic intention (bodhicitta): the mind dedicated to attaining enlightenment in order to benefit all others most effectively.

Arhat: a person who has attained liberation and is free from cyclic existence.

Arya: a person who has realized emptiness directly and is thus one of the Sangha Jewels of refuge.

Bodhisattva: a person who has developed the spontaneous altruistic intention.

Buddha: any person who has purified all defilements and developed all good qualities. "The Buddha" refers to Shakyamuni Buddha, who lived 2,500 years ago in India.

Buddhist deity: a manifestation of the enlightened minds appearing in a physical form.

Buddha nature (Buddha potential): the innate qualities of the mind enabling all beings to attain enlightenment.

Compassion: the wish for all sentient beings to be free from suffering and its causes.

Concentration: the ability to remain single-pointedly on the object of meditation.

Cyclic existence (samsara): uncontrollably being reborn under the influence of disturbing attitudes and karmic imprints.

Determination to be free: the attitude of aspiring to be free from all problems and sufferings and to attain liberation.

Dharma: the wisdom realizing emptiness, and the absence of suffering and its causes that this wisdom brings. In a more general sense, Dharma refers to the teachings and doctrine of the Buddha.

Disturbing attitudes and negative emotions: attitudes and emotions, such as ignorance, attachment, anger, pride, jealousy, and closed-mindedness, that disturb our mental peace and propel us to act in ways harmful to ourselves and others.

Empowerment (initiation): a ceremony in Vajrayana Buddhism after which the disciple is permitted to meditate on a particular manifestation of the Buddha.

Emptiness: the lack of independent or inherent existence. This is the ultimate nature or reality of all persons and phenomena.

Enlightenment (Buddhahood): the state of a Buddha, i.e. the state of having forever eliminated all obscurations from the mindstream, and having developed our good qualities and wisdom to their fullest extent. Buddhahood supersedes liberation.

Fantasized ways of existing: see Inherent or independent existence.

Imprint: the residual energy left on the mindstream when an action has been completed. When it matures, it influences our experience. Imprints generally refer to karmic seeds.

Inherent, or independent, existence: a false and nonexistent quality that we project onto persons and phenomena; existence independent of causes and conditions, parts, or the mind labeling a phenomena.

Initiation: see Empowerment.

Karma: intentional action. Our actions leave imprints on our mindstreams, which bring about our experiences.

Liberation: freedom from cyclic existence.

Love: the wish for all sentient beings to have happiness and its causes.

Mahayana: the Buddhist tradition that asserts that all beings can attain enlightenment. It strongly emphasizes the development of compassion and the altruistic intention.

Mantra: a series of syllables consecrated by a Buddha that express the essence of the entire path to enlightenment. They are recited to concentrate and purify the mind.

Meditation: habituating ourselves to positive attitudes and correct perspectives.

Mind: the experiential, cognitive part of living beings. Formless, the mind isn't made of atoms, nor is it perceivable through our five senses.

Mindstream: the continuity of the mind.

Monk: a celibate male ordained practitioner.

Nirvana: the cessation of unsatisfactory conditions and their causes.

Nun: a celibate female ordained practitioner.

Ordination: taking the precepts set out by the Buddha to restrain from destructive actions. There are various levels of ordination for both lay people and monastics, but in general the term is used to refer to the taking of precepts by monks and nuns.

Positive potential: imprints of positive actions, which will result in happiness in the future. Sometimes translated as "merit" or "good karma."

Precepts (vows): guidelines set out by the Buddha to help us refrain from destructive actions.

Priest: non-celibate Buddhist clergy from certain Japanese Buddhist traditions.

Pure Land: a Mahayana Buddhist tradition emphasizing methods to gain rebirth in a pure land. A pure land is a place established by a Buddha or bodhisattva where all conditions are conducive for the practice of Dharma and the attainment of enlightenment.

Realization: a clear, deep, and correct understanding of what the Buddha taught. This may be either conceptual or nonconceptual direct experience. The nonconceptual direct realizations gained at higher levels of the path cleanse the obscurations from our minds forever.

Sangha: any person who directly and nonconceptually realizes emptiness. In a more general sense, sangha refers to the communities of ordained monks and nuns. It sometimes is used to refer to Buddhists in general.

Selflessness: see Emptiness.

Special insight (vipassana): discriminating analytical wisdom. Special insight into emptiness realizes the empty nature of phenomena.

Suffering (duhkha): any dissatisfactory condition. This doesn't refer only to physical or mental pain, but includes all problematic and unsatisfactory conditions.

Taking refuge: entrusting our spiritual development to the guidance of the Buddhas, Dharma, and Sangha.

Tantra: a scripture describing a Vajrayana practice. This term can also refer to the Vajrayana practice itself.

Theravada: the Tradition of the Elders, a Buddhist tradition widespread in Southeast Asia and Sri Lanka.

Three Jewels: the Buddhas, Dharma, and Sangha.

Vajrayana: a Mahayana Buddhist tradition popular in Tibet and Japan.

Vow: see Precepts.

Wisdom realizing reality (wisdom realizing emptiness, wisdom realizing the lack of fantasized ways of existing): a mind that correctly understands the manner in which all persons and phenomena exist, i.e., the mind realizing the emptiness of inherent existence.

Zen (Ch'an): a Mahayana Buddhist tradition popular in China and Japan.

FURTHER READING

Berzin, Alexander. *Relating to a Spiritual Teacher: Building a Healthy Relationship*. Ithaca: Snow Lion, 2000.

Chodron, Thubten. *Blossoms of the Dharma: Living as a Buddhist Nun*. Berkeley: North Atlantic Books, 2000.

———. *Open Heart, Clear Mind*. Ithaca: Snow Lion, 1990.

———. *Taming the Monkey Mind*. Heian: Torrance, 1999.

The Dalai Lama, H.H., Tenzin Gyatso. *Kindness, Clarity and Insight*. Ithaca: Snow Lion, 1984.

———. *The Dalai Lama at Harvard*. trans. by Jeffrey Hopkins. Ithaca: Snow Lion, 1989.

Dhammananda, K. Sri. *How to Live Without Fear and Worry*. Kuala Lumpur: Buddhist Missionary Society, 1989.

———. *What Buddhists Believe*. Kuala Lumpur: Buddhist Missionary Society, 1987.

Dhammananda, K. Sri, ed. *The Dhammapada*. Kuala Lumpur: Sasana Abhiwurdhi Wardhana Society, 1988.

Dharmaraksita. *Wheel of Sharp Weapons*. Dharamsala: Library of Tibetan Works and Archives, 1981.

Dilgo Khyentse Rinpoche. *Enlightened Courage*. Ithaca: Snow Lion, 1993.

Eppsteiner, Fred, ed. *Path of Compassion*. Berkeley: Parallax, 1988.

Gampopa. *The Jewel Ornament of Liberation*. trans. by Herbert Guenther. Boulder: Shambhala, 1971.

Goldstein, Joseph. *The Experience of Insight*. Boston: Shambhala, 1987.

Hanh, Thich Nhat. *Being Peace*. Berkeley: Parallax, 1988.

Kapleau, Philip, ed. *The Three Pillars of Zen*. London: Rider, 1980.

Khema, Ayya. *Being Nobody, Going Nowhere*. Boston: Wisdom, 1987.

Kornfield, Jack and Breiter, Paul, ed. *A Still Forest Pool*. Wheaton: Theosophical Publishing House, 1987.

Longchenpa. *Kindly Bent to Ease Us*. trans. by Herbert Guenther. Emeryville: Dharma, 1978.

McDonald, Kathleen. *How to Meditate*. Boston: Wisdom, 1984.

Nyanaponika, Thera. *Heart of Buddhist Meditation*. London: Rider, 1962.

Rabten, Geshe and Dhargye, Geshe. *Advice from a Spiritual Friend*. Boston: Wisdom, 1986.

Rinchen, Geshe Sonam and Sonam, Ruth. *Thirty-seven Practices of Bodhisattvas*. Ithaca: Snow Lion, 1996.

Schumann, H.W. *The Historical Buddha*. London: Arkana, 1989.

Sparham, Gareth, trans. *Tibetan Dhammapada*. Boston: Wisdom, 1983.

Stevenson, Ian. *Cases of the Reincarnation Type*. Charlottesville: University of Virginia Press, 1975. (4 vol.)

Story, Francis. *Rebirth as Doctrine and Experience*. Kandy: Buddhist Publication Society, 1975.

Suzuki, D. T. *An Introduction to Zen Buddhism*. London: Rider, 1969.

Suzuki, Shunriyu. *Zen Mind, Beginner's Mind*. New York: Weatherhill, 1980.

Tegchog, Geshe Jampa. *Transforming the Heart: The Buddhist Way to Joy and Courage*. Ithaca: Snow Lion, 1999.

Trungpa, Chogyam. *Cutting Through Spiritual Materialism*. London: Shambhala, 1973.

Tsomo, Karma Lekshe, ed. *Daughters of the Buddha*. Ithaca: Snow Lion, 1988.

Tsongkhapa, Je. *The Three Principal Aspects of the Path.* Howell: Mahayana Sutra and Tantra Press, 1988.

Wangchen, Geshe. *Awakening the Mind of Enlightenment.* Boston: Wisdom, 1988.

Willis, Janice D. ed. *Feminine Ground.* Ithaca: Snow Lion, 1987.

Yeshe, Lama Thubten, *Introduction to Tantra.* Boston: Wisdom, 1987.

Zopa Rinpoche. *Door to Satisfaction.* Boston: Wisdom, 1994.

———. *Transforming Problems: Utilizing Happiness and Suffering in the Spiritual Path.* Boston: Wisdom, 1987.

RESOURCES

The list below is not exhaustive of all the resources available. Each organization listed below should be able to put you in touch with similar organizations in your area.

For information on socially engaged Buddhism:

Buddhist Peace Fellowship, Box 4650, Berkeley CA 94704, U.S.A.

For information on women and Buddhism:

Sakyadhita (Daughters of the Buddha), 400 Hobron Lane #2615, Honolulu HI 96815, U.S.A.

Yasodhara newsletter, c/o Dr. Chatsumarn Kabilsingh, Faculty of Liberal Arts, Thammat University, Bangkok 10200, Thailand

For Buddhist materials for children:

Department of Buddhist Education, Buddhist Churches of America, 1710 Octavia St., San Francisco CA 94109, U.S.A. (They produce the cartoon video, "The Life of the Buddha" in three parts and have Sunday School material.)

Dharma Press, 2425 Hillside Ave., Berkeley CA 94704, U.S.A.

Snow Lion Publications, Box 6483, Ithaca NY 14851, U.S.A.

For listings of Buddhist temples and centers:

Coleman, Graham, ed. *A Handbook of Tibetan Culture.* Boston: Shambhala, 1994.

Moreale, Don. *Buddhist America.* Santa Fe NM: John Muir Publications, 1988.

http://www.Dharmanet.org   (Dharma Net International)

http://www.fpmt.org   (Foundation for the Preservation of the Mahayana Tradition)

For interreligious dialogue:

American Buddhist Congress, 933 S. New Hampshire Ave., Los Angeles CA 90006, U.S.A.

Chodron, Thubten, ed., *Interfaith Insights.* New Delhi : Timeless Books, 2000.

Council for a Parliament of the World's Religions, P.O. Box 1630, Chicago IL 60690-1630, U.S.A.